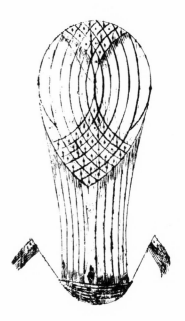

Graven by the fishermen themselves

SCRIMSHAW IN MYSTIC SEAPORT MUSEUM

RICHARD C. MALLEY

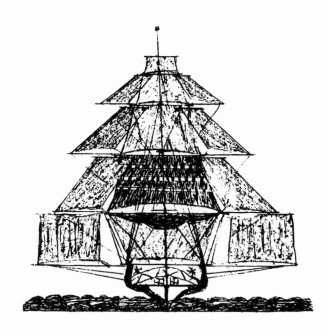

Mystic Seaport Museum, Inc., Mystic, Connecticut 1983

This monograph has been published through a generous
grant from the Andrew W. Mellon Foundation.

Acc. nos. 39.860, 39.875, 39.878, 39.883, from the collection
of the New England Savings Bank, on loan to Mystic Seaport
Musum, are reproduced with the permission of the lender.

COVER: Engraved panbone whaling scene (see also color plate I,
facing p. 80).

FIRST PRINTING, 1983

Cataloging in Publication Data
Mystic Seaport Museum, Inc., Mystic, Conn.
   Graven by the fishermen themselves: Scrimshaw
in Mystic Seaport Museum, by Richard C. Malley.
Mystic, 1983.
   156 p. illus., 4 col. plates. 22 cm.
1. Scrimshaw – Mystic Seaport Museum – Catalogs.
I. Malley, Richard C., 1952-
NK 6022.M9
ISBN: 0-913372-27-7

Printed in the United States of America

TO MY PARENTS

CONTENTS

FOREWORD

In 1980 the Andrew W. Mellon Foundation made a grant to Mystic Seaport Museum for the purpose of making information about our collection available both to the public and to scholars. Given this opportunity for funding research and publication, we decided to publish a series of monographs, each covering in depth one area of the collection or field of interest. It is appropriate, because of its quality and extent, that the scrimshaw collection inaugurate this series.

This collection reflects decades of care and connoisseurship by private collectors and museum staff members. As the author points out, the scrimshaw collection at Mystic Seaport received two remarkable installments in the early years, one from the Mariners Savings Bank in New London (now the New England Savings Bank) and another from an individual, Charles E. White, son of a New London shipmaster. Both collections were developed in an era when the items could be obtained directly from the whalers themselves or their families. There was no question of authenticity, and as these and other early donors to the museum built their collections they became more discerning and acquired the fine works of folk art that ultimately gave their collections great distinction.

From these artifacts, now at the Seaport, we can sense some of the joy the donors must have felt as collectors. As visitors looking at the pieces, as staff members working with them, and as readers of this book, we can appreciate the interest that arises when these objects are carefully studied and the fascination that increases as a greater knowledge of the origins, methods, sources of scenes, and identities of artists is acquired.

One staff member has been at the focal point of the collection for more than seven years. Richard C. Malley, Assistant Registrar, has examined and cataloged all new acquisitions of scrimshaw during this period, updated the records on hundreds of other pieces, studied every scrimshaw item in the collection, and published and lectured on the subject. From this background he has emerged as the ideal author for this book. We hope that the information contained here will stimulate more research that will further enrich scholarship in the field.

I would like to extend my thanks to the Andrew W. Mellon Foundation, the scrimshanders, the collectors, the donors, the curators, and the museum staff, past and present, for creating the collection and for bringing this volume into existence. Particular appreciation goes to Richard Malley for sharing his knowledge and quiet enthusiasm with all of us.

The superb scrimshaw at Mystic Seaport Museum warrants the attention of visitors and scholars and through this publication will become known to a wider audience. Reading this book should inspire admiration for the handiwork of the sailor/artists and a respect for the collectors who have handed it down to us.

J. Revell Carr, *Director*

ACKNOWLEDGMENTS

Title pages often mislead by hiding the fact that nearly every publication is, in reality, the collaborative effort of many individuals. This study is no exception.

The Andrew W. Mellon Foundation made the publication of this monograph possible through a generous grant to Mystic Seaport Museum. Special research and technical assistance were provided by the following people: Mrs. Thomas Adams and John Bockstoce of the New Bedford Whaling Museum, John S. Carter of the Maine Maritime Museum, Paul Cyr of the New Bedford Free Public Library, Robert Ellis and Stuart M. Frank of the Kendall Whaling Museum, William Gilkerson, Louis H. Hollister, Constance P. Ramstedt, Edouard A. Stackpole of the Nantucket Whaling Museum, Joseph Szaszfai of the Yale University Art Gallery, and Paul Winfisky of the Peabody Museum. Thanks are due Klaus Gemming for his fine design. I am especially indebted to John O. Sands of the Mariners Museum for reading the manuscript; his comments and encouragement were of great help.

In addition I would like to thank the New England Savings Bank, Mrs. Alexander O. Vietor, The Dietrich Brothers Americana Corporation and in particular their curator, Alexandra W. Rollins, and assistant curator, Deborah M. Rebuck, Dr. Oscar Hollander, and Robert J. Narkis for their cooperation.

Closer to home numerous colleagues on the museum staff deserve special mention. I wish to thank J. Revell Carr, Director, for his encouragement and suggestions during the preparation of this work. Anne M. Preuss, project editor, has been of immeasurable aid in guiding the progress of the monograph. Claire White-Peterson and Mary Anne Stets of the photographic staff are unsung heroes in the production of this study and deserve special thanks. The reference and manuscript staffs of the G. W. Blunt White Library have been very understanding in the face of special requests during the course of research. Thanks are also due to the following staff members: Jessie Baker, Philip L. Budlong, Fred Calabretta, Benjamin A. G. Fuller, Curator, Andrew W. German, Rodi Hamilton, Martin Hillsgrove, Jane Massett, David F. Mathieson, Elizabeth Parker, William N. Peterson, and Nancy Zercher.

Finally I wish to express my very personal thanks to Lisa Halttunen, valued colleague and good friend, whose ready encouragement and sound advice contributed so much to the writing of this work.

Richard C. Malley

After graduating from Providence College in 1974 Richard C. Malley received his M. A. in American history from Fordham University. A member of the Curatorial Department at Mystic Seaport Museum since 1976, he is currently Assistant Registrar.

Throughout the Pacific, and also in Nantucket, and New Bedford, and Sag Harbor, you will come across lively sketches of whales and whaling-scenes, graven by the fishermen themselves on Sperm Whale-teeth, or ladies' busks wrought out of the Right Whale-bone, and other like skrimshander articles, as the whalemen call the numerous little ingenious contrivances they elaborately carve out of the rough material, in their hours of ocean leisure.

Herman Melville, *Moby-Dick*, Chapter LVII

A NOTE ON DESCRIPTIONS

Every effort has been made to describe accurately the scrimshaw items mentioned in this monograph. Measurements have been made to the nearest sixteenth of an inch. Unless otherwise specified the measurement noted in each caption is the largest.

Chapter 1 *Scrimshaw: An Introduction*

Ask a dozen people to define scrimshaw, and you will probably get as many different answers. For in spite of scrimshaw's current popularity, the word means different things to different people. Happily, this divergence of opinion is a matter of degree rather than of substance, of narrow versus broad interpretations.

Everyone agrees that whaling, and especially the cast-off by-products of that brutal business, is central to any reasonable definition. But here the fun really begins. What about materials from other creatures like the walrus and porpoise? Is scrimshaw strictly American? Did scrimshaw end with the demise of large-scale American whaling? What about materials like wood and shell?

Clearly no single definition of the word scrimshaw will suit everyone; so for guidance let's fall back on the whole *raison d'être* for this monograph – Mystic Seaport Museum's extensive scrimshaw collection. Based on the holdings in the Museum, a reasonable definition could go something like this: "Scrimshaw is the activity of carving or engraving on the ivory, bone, and other by-products of certain marine mammals, and the use of these same materials in the fashioning of home-made items."

An overview of the collection would further tell us that scrimshaw appears to be largely an American phenomenon, primarily nineteenth century in time and character, and closely associated with seafarers, especially whalemen. Further, while whale and walrus products are almost always utilized, secondary materials like wood and shell are also commonly found. Other generalizations could be noted, such as the naive or untrained ("primitive" has too pejorative a connotation) quality of much of the decorative work, or the often astounding ingenuity of the many handmade contrivances.

The fact that the collection numbers about eight hundred pieces precludes a study of each and every item. Rather, an attempt will be made to examine the major types of pieces and design styles. Items typifying the various categories of decorative and utilitarian scrimshaw will be discussed and illustrated, along with some of the more extraordinary examples in the collection. It is hoped that this approach will afford the reader at once an appreciation of the wide range of work produced and the degree of artistic achievement possible.

Eskimo carvings have not been included in this work, it being felt that they are better left to an ethnographic study. Likewise, the hazy area of "allied arts," like military powder horns, prisoner-of-war models and carvings, Nantucket lightship baskets, sailor's valentines, and other shellwork, has been excluded.

What's in a Word?

Whether a certain definition of scrimshaw is broad or narrow, one point is clear: "scrimshaw" denotes both an activity and the result, or product, of that activity.

Less than clear, however, is the derivation of the word itself. There are about as many theories concerning the origin of the word "scrimshaw" as there are definitions of that term. The arguments, far too long for a work of this length, are neatly summarized in Chapter 1 of E. Norman Flayderman's *Scrimshaw and Scrimshanders* published in 1972. As it would be redundant to retrace that author's extensive research, let's simply note some of the more widely held theories discussed in that fine work, which is, unfortunately, out of print and nigh impossible to find.

An 1853 work accords "scrimpshoning" a low Dutch parentage, the term roughly meaning labor for basically decorative purposes. An American Indian connection is suggested in *The Island of Nantucket* (1882) where it is maintained that "skrimshonting" is a bastardized form of an Indian word having to do with a type of carving. Clifford W. Ashley in his 1926 work, *The Yankee Whaler,* dwells, not surprisingly, on a Yankee origin: the word "scrimp" can be taken as meaning "to economize," a necessity if one has only a limited supply of raw material like whale teeth. Flayderman himself suggests that "shaw" might be traced back to the verbs "to saw" and "to sand." Together the words could denote an economical activity, which is an apt description of the art. Rounding out the major theories is that one which indicates a connection to the British military slang term "scrimshank," suggestive of malingering or avoiding work.[1]

Perhaps the most interesting wrinkle in the etymological debate was added by a Cleveland attorney who firmly held that scrimshaw is actually a corrupted form of the term "skirmisher," an Old English expression for the Norse warriors who regularly raided England in the eighth and ninth centuries. It seems that in the doldrums between assaults these "skirmishers" occupied themselves with, among other things, an occasional whaling

venture; and some even whiled away idle hours carving lacy designs on whalebone and teeth. And these Norse designs also later came to be known as "scrimshaw." The argument appeared all the more convincing when one considered the proponent's name – Charles W. Scrimshaw.[2]

The variety of spellings of the word scrimshaw observed in the previous paragraphs represents only a small sampling. Its earliest known use in a period document appears in the log of the 99-ton whaling brig *Orion* of Rochester, Massachusetts, Captain Obed Luce, on 14 March 1821:

First and Middle part these 24 hours calm. Latter part light breezes and pleasant weather. all hands employed scrimshonting. so ends this day. – – – – no Whales and hard times."[3]

Luce's last remark refers to the *Orion*'s miserable luck in catching only five sperm whales after nine months of cruising the Atlantic.

Undoubtedly mispronunciation, a lack of schooling, and the seeming nineteenth-century aversion to spelling a word the same way twice if it could be helped contributed to these and other variations such as "scrimshorn, scrinshorn, schrimson, schrimpshong, skrimshontering, and squimshon."[4]

Ivory Carving in Antiquity

At the time of the earliest development of the particular nautical art known as scrimshaw, mid-eighteenth-century American whalemen were, unconsciously, carrying on an activity dating back possibly as far as 20,000 B.C., when hunters carved or engraved the mammoth's tusks.[5] Certainly the ancient Egyptians were noted for their carving of hippopotamus teeth, a feat rarely copied by nineteenth-century whalemen. Among the first people known to use whale ivory were the seagoing Phoenicians, who by about the first millennium B.C. were venturing beyond the Pillars of Hercules and into the open Atlantic. It is said that they actually preferred whale teeth to any other type of ivory for their best carvings.[6] Europeans were active in the carving of ivory, from the very early Middle Ages. On the other side of the globe ivory carving was well established in the Orient, especially in China and India where, believe it or not, walrus ivory was all the rage.

Other cultures, like those of the Pacific islands and of the peoples of northern Asia and North America, were active in ivory carving, the former using whale teeth and the latter walrus tusks and seal teeth. Thus, while scrimshaw is described as primarily American in origin, it is not without parallels in other times and places.

At the same time certain characteristics distinguish scrimshaw from these earlier carvings, as we shall see. Such factors as a brief period of activity, a very narrow group of practitioners, a less-than-perfect artistic environment, an incredible multiplicity of finished works, and an unusual motivation, escape from boredom, serve to place this activity apart from other ivory carving traditions.

Whaling and Scrimshaw

The practice of scrimshaw can be said to be a direct result of American whaling and the individual whaleman's role in that industry, and a brief survey of the whale fishery is crucial for placing scrimshaw in its proper context.

Early whaling off America's coast was shore-based, with small boats setting off from land after locally migrating whales. The captured animals were then processed back on the beach.

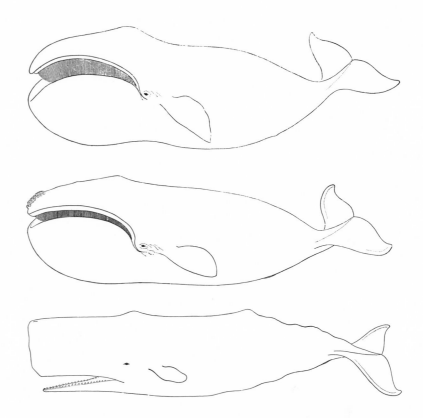

1. Among the species most often sought by American whalemen were, top to bottom, the bowhead whale, the right whale, and the sperm whale. Note the baleen in the mouths of the first two species. From *The Fisheries and Fishery Industries of the United States*, 1884.

By the seventeenth century vessels were hunting both bowhead and right whales [1] far offshore, but here again the actual "trying out" of the blubber into oil was done once the whalers returned home from a cruise. The subsequent discovery of valuable sperm whales [1] well off the coast early in the eighteenth century contributed to the development of pelagic whaling as the primary mode of operation.

· 17 ·

After the upheaval of the Revolution, American whalemen began to voyage farther afield and in larger vessels, pursuing the wide-ranging sperm whale into the Pacific and Indian oceans as early as 1791. Following the disruption of the War of 1812, American whaling entered a period of unprecedented growth and prosperity that saw voyages into nearly every sea where whales were to be found, even hostile arctic waters. By the late 1850s the American fleet numbered over 700 vessels; New Bedford alone listed 329 in 1857.[7] One estimate puts at twenty thousand the number of men engaged in this industry in any year during the period 1825-1865; perhaps there were one hundred fifty thousand or more American whalemen during this so-called "Golden Age of Whaling."[8]

A series of random events rapidly altered the fortunes of this boom industry. Alternative materials for lighting and lubrication, notably coal gas and petroleum distillates, quickly reduced the demand for whale oil lubricants and lamp oil, as well as for spermaceti candles. Losses of Yankee whaleships to Confederate commerce raiders during the Civil War were devastating. A series of postwar disasters further decimated the fleet: treacherous arctic pack ice claimed dozens of vessels in 1871 and again in 1876. In addition, overhunting had seriously depleted some key whale stocks.

Curiously, the demand for baleen, a flexible material found in such whale species as the right and bowhead, increased as this nineteenth-century "plastic" was adapted to a variety of commercial uses, most notably in the fashion industry where it was used in corsets and collars. But even this revival could not forestall the precipitous decline of American whaling, which industry died quietly early in this century.

Why Scrimshaw?

Whaling is one thing as seen from the counting house, but quite another from the vantage point of the fo'c'sle, which is from where we must view it to understand the development of scrimshaw.

During the nineteenth century whaling voyages were measured in years, not months. Given the great distances involved and the ability to try out blubber on board, a vessel did not normally return home until the hold was full. Whether the quarry was the large sperm whale with its high-grade oil and valuable spermaceti, or its smaller, gentler cousins the bowhead and right whales, the routine was the same: "Hurry up and wait." A month or more might pass between kills, and in the meantime there was only so much shipboard work to keep thirty men occupied.

Boredom was more than a minor annoyance; it became a fact of life and a major shipboard problem. Confiding in his diary, an American whaleman cruising off the coast of Japan in 1843 lamented: "I hope we'll see sperm whales soon. If we don't, I don't know but what I shall go off the handle."[9] Close quarters, and fairly grim ones at that, compounded the problem of unremitting boredom.

Under such conditions it is only logical to expect a variety of pastimes to have emerged. Fancy carpentry engaged some; others found an outlet in decorative ropework. But among the whalemen scrimshaw became the most popular channel for pent-up energy, both physical and creative.

In addition to providing "busy work" and a safety valve for emotional pressures, scrimshaw produced a trophy, a relic, a souvenir, or what have you, of this often dangerous employment. Of particular significance was the sperm whale tooth, which Flayderman has compared with a bull's ear,[10] both trophies bespeaking courage and skill. For, whatever social graces the whaleman lacked, fortitude and daring were to be found aplenty aboard whaling vessels. These were the qualities that counted.

Scrimshaw required time, and the whaleman had plenty of this to spare. In this regard a whaling voyage has even been compared to a jail term.[11] Scrimshaw required certain raw materials, and the cast-off by-products of whaling were usually available. Scrimshaw required some manual skill, and expertise with a jackknife was part and parcel of any shipboard duty. These key factors combined with a pressing need for time-killing diversion, resulting in the widespread shipboard practice of what we call scrimshaw.

Given the fact that seamen of all nations labored under many of the same conditions, and that some nations likewise hunted whales, it is interesting to note that scrimshaw is found mostly aboard American vessels. This is not to say that only American citizens pursued this hobby, for in time men of other races and nationalities shipped aboard American whaleships. As the nineteenth century wore on, crews became less "Yankee" in their makeup, yet scrimshaw continued to be practiced.

It is particularly curious to note that the British, who had a whale fleet of respectable size, did not produce more scrimshaw than they did. Certain obvious factors contributing to this situation include the relatively small number of British whalers as compared to the hundreds of vessels from American ports; the generally shorter voyages conducted by British whaleships; and the fact that they pursued the bowhead and right whales more often than the toothed sperm whale. One English observer noted that scrimshaw "is not much done by British or other sailors, but…on American ships is pursued by white Christian and Coloured Pagan with equal avidness."[12]

One writer has recently attributed the lack of foreign, especially British, scrimshaw to the prevailing class system, whereby the usually middle- or upper-class shipmaster did not share the ordinary seaman's taste or need for such "nonproductive" diversions. This attitude was often at variance with that of his American counterpart, who normally began his career in the fo'c'sle.[13] Indeed, the scrimshanding productivity of Captain Fred Smith of the New Bedford bark *Ohio,* for example, seems astounding (see chapters 2 and 4). One wonders if he had much time for hunting whales during his several voyages, so many and varied were the apparent fruits of his cabin-bound labor.

Another explanation for the apparent lack of British scrimshaw is the possibility that much of it may not be recognized as such. A tooth incised with the popular view of the War of 1812 battle between frigates H.M.S. *Shannon* and U.S.S. *Chesapeake,* for example, could certainly be a British trophy. They did win *that* one, after all. Equally valid is the possibility that some of the pieces engraved with fashionable ladies are not necessarily American. The latest fashions, remember, were almost always European, soon to catch the eyes of women in America. And geometric patterns are universally popular. Therefore the British and European contributions to this art, though certainly far less than the American, might be greater than believed.

Scrimshaw was not confined exclusively to whaleships. Merchant sailors produced some fine examples of the art, even though they did not have as much spare time or as ready access to the basic raw materials as the whalemen. Seamen in both the American and British navies are also known to have pursued scrimshaw, sometimes in spite of standing orders to the contrary. And let's not forget the occasional piece produced by women on shipboard.

At the root of the problem of identifying the origin of a scrimshaw item is the fact that so few pieces can be traced to a particular individual or vessel. The anonymous nature of scrimshaw is often noted in describing the practice as a "folk art." But what else characterizes folk art? And how else does scrimshaw qualify for this term?

Scrimshaw as Folk Art

Clifford W. Ashley, whaleman, artist, and author of *The Yankee Whaler* (1926) called scrimshaw "the only important indigenous folk art, except that of the Indians, we have ever had in America."[14] He apparently felt that, unlike other folk art forms that were transplanted from Europe or elsewhere, scrimshaw was an art more strictly American in origin, shaped in large measure by the living and working conditions of the American whaleman. "Folk art" can be literally translated as "people's art," that is, art by the people and art for the people. Scrimshaw was done by the whaleman and primarily for the whaleman, as an alternative to *ennui*. He was not motivated by profit, though sperm whale teeth could double as currency in exchange for supplies and "favors" on certain Pacific islands; and a few waterfront establishments in port cities might accept a piece in return for a meal or a bed.[15] But considering the fairly slow pace of scrimshawing this would not have been a profitable undertaking at the time.

The other general exception to the "personal" nature of scrimshaw was the occasional piece intended for a close friend or relative. The elaborate jagging wheel or pie crimper and the decorated corset busk, both intended for a wife or "the girl he left behind," are prime examples of this practice. At least one of Frederick Myrick's now famous "*Susan*'s teeth," executed by him on board the whaler *Susan* in the late 1820s, is engraved as being intended "For Mr. Prince Coffin." But again, these items appear to be more the exception than the rule.

The fact that the vast majority of scrimshaw works are unsigned lends weight to the argument that scrimshaw was largely done for the benefit of the artist himself.[16] And one of the characteristics of folk art in general is that the product was normally intended for "home consumption," which in this case could mean both the fo'c'sle at sea and the front parlor ashore.

Folk art is normally associated with a lack of formal academic training. Frederick Myrick, the whaleman creator of the exquisite "*Susan*'s teeth," appears to have had some training as an engraver, and possibly worked at that trade at some time in his life. W. L. Roderick, who produced a number of fine teeth on board the British bark *Adventure* in 1852, also seems to have had some engraving experience. But men like these represent a tiny minority of the thousands of scrimshanders. More commonly found are the many freehand scenes that tend to be a bit on the flat side and lack proper perspective, exposing their creator's lack of artistic training. All the same, their work is considered better than period Eskimo engraving, for example, in terms of sophistication and artistic technique.[17]

Scrimshaw was a vital art in the sense that there was no rigid boundary beyond which the artist could not tread. The many subject matters and decorative motifs attest to this fact. How else could the creation of the many dozens of different objects utilizing such varied styles be explained? Certainly there is no denying that illustrated material was used by many, if not most, scrimshanders to some degree.[18] But as ex-whaleman Ashley argues, his isolation virtually forced the scrimshander to develop original and varied styles of work at some point during the voyage.[19] Only in instances where published illustrations were slavishly followed is there any real sameness among the work. This is particularly true in the case of women's portraits and some naval battle scenes. But even here individual styles of detailing and coloring serve to offset much of the similarity.

Scrimshaw has been called a unique form of folk art for a number of reasons. First, many of the tools needed to practice the art had to be made by the scrimshander himself. Saws and files were often formed from strips of heated iron. And a nail or sail needle, for example, worked better as an engraving tool if equipped with a handle of wood or even whalebone.[20] Second, the primary motivation for the art was not so much a wish to produce something wonderful as it was to avoid something awful, namely, unbearable boredom. To top off things, it's hard to imagine more trying circumstances under which to produce such art as those found in a crowded fo'c'sle or on a pitching deck. But this is where most scrimshaw was produced.

Evidence seems to indicate that once ashore the whaleman or sailor was less inclined to practice the art.[21] This helps explain why the amount of scrimshaw declined along with the fortunes of the American whaling industry in the late nineteenth century.

Whether or not scrimshaw is the only indigenous American folk art developed is probably less certain, and less important perhaps, than the fact that it is undoubtedly an art by and for the people, and one conceived because of, and in spite of, certain conditions peculiar to America's maritime experience.

Materials . . .

Of value in any basic study of scrimshaw is a rudimentary knowledge of the raw materials utilized by the scrimshander, and, by extension, some understanding of the physiology of certain marine mammals. For it is only through an awareness of the physical characteristics and limitations of these materials that the artistic and craft achievements of the scrimshander can be fully appreciated.

"Whale ivory" has become synonymous with the large teeth of the sperm whale. Though other flesh-eating whales like the beluga and the killer whales have teeth, only the sperm whale was commercially hunted on a large scale. The sperm's long lower jaw, which in an adult can approach twenty feet in length, contains anywhere from twenty to fifty teeth [2], ranging in length from about five to ten inches each.[22] The upper jaw is supplied with tough, sheathlike slots into which these impressive teeth fit when the creature closes its enormous mouth.

Few laymen today know that ivory is "an organic matrix impregnated with calcareous salts and permeated with exceedingly fine tubes starting at the pulp and radiating outward."[23] Probably even fewer care that only elephant tusks are considered true ivory. Certainly this would have made little difference to the scrimshander as he selected a tooth for engraving. For our purposes let's define ivory as a hard, opaque, creamy white substance with a fine grain.

In their natural state, whale teeth are heavily ridged and hollow for about half their length. Normal wear of the enamel at the tips often exposes a circular patch of the slightly pinkish underlying dentin [3]. There tends to be variety in overall size and shape, some teeth being broad, others more narrow and pointed.

Whalebone from the skeleton also serves as a potential raw material for the scrimshander. The usual source of whalebone is the huge lower jaw of the sperm whale [4], which is quite often flat and thin, especially near the hinges, ideal for cutting into slabs of different shapes. In addition this "panbone," as it's termed, is not nearly so coarsely grained as other portions of the skeleton, making it applicable to both decorative and construction purposes.

The suborder of whales *Mysticeti,* which includes the right whale and the bowhead or "Greenland right" whale, could also provide the shipbound artist with suitable material for his

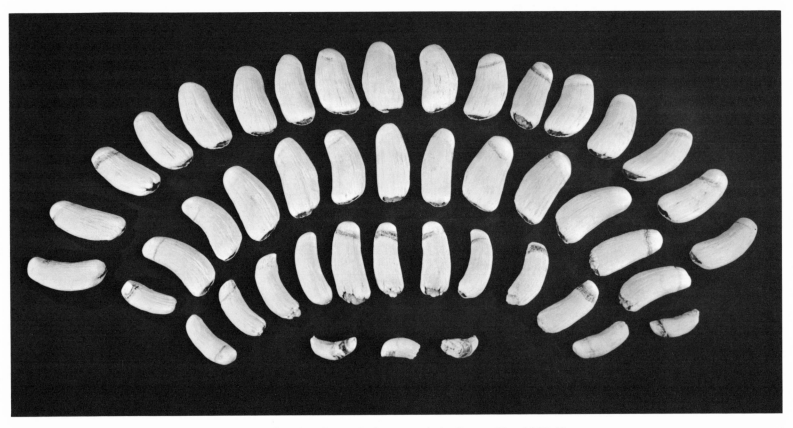

2. Note the variety in size and shape of these teeth, taken from a bull sperm whale. *Source:* Harold H. Kynett, 65.889.1-45

off-duty diversion. Unlike the sperm whale, these animals are filter feeders, harvesting krill and other plankton through an ingenious straining system of large overlapping baleen plates. After admitting a mouthful of food and water the whales force the water out through these flexible, hair-fringed plates, effectively trapping the food, which is then ingested.

Attached to the roof of the mouth, these plates range anywhere from two to twelve feet in length. Just one of these

"baleen whales," as they are collectively called, may boast more than three thousand pounds of this substance, which, depending on the species, can range in color from mud brown to a green-yellow hue. Composed largely of keratin, a fibrous protein found in human nails and hair, baleen was seized upon by the scrimshanders for its resilient and malleable qualities, useful in a variety of applications.

With increased penetration of arctic waters by whalers after

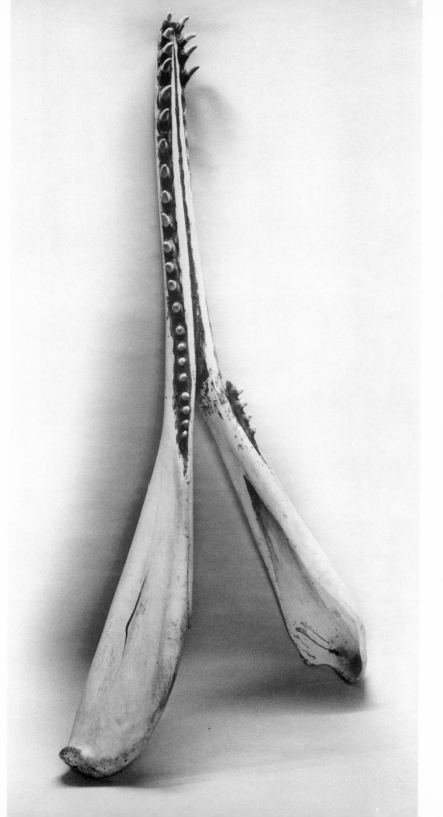

3. Closeup of a raw sperm whale tooth exhibiting characteristic wear at the tip, 9 in. (22.9 cm.). *Source:* New England Savings Bank, 39.878

4. The lower jaw of a small sperm whale, clearly illustrating the flat "panbone" near the hinges, 7 ft. 2 in. (218.4 cm.). *Source:* Robert Breeding, 80.21

the 1830s, walrus tusks, normally purchased from Eskimos, became a useful medium for the scrimshander's art. These tusks are in fact the upper incisor teeth of the animal [5], which, in the male, can exceed thirty inches in length. Though more coarsely grained than whale ivory, these tusks would nonetheless provide a large working surface for decorative purposes, and long straight pieces for various scrimshaw contrivances. Walrus tusks, incidentally, are characterized by a crystalline core resembling quartz [6]; this trademark is often visible in walrus ivory objects. Many of these tusks have been pierced through at the tip, a procedure that, according to John Bockstoce of the New Bedford Whaling Museum, allowed each pair to be tied

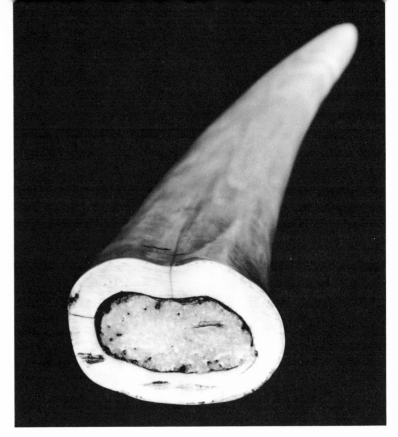

6. Detail from a small walrus tusk. Note the quartzlike core material. *Source:* Estate of Bradley H. Barnes, 73.421

5. The tusks of the Pacific walrus supplied raw material for many scrimshanders. From *The Fisheries and Fishing Industries of the United States,* 1884.

together and placed on the hook of a spring scale when being weighed for trade.[24]

Less frequently available were materials from other marine creatures. Teeth from seals or sea lions were only rarely used by scrimshanders, especially in view of their small size. Occasionally the jawbone of a harpooned porpoise was utilized for some decorative purpose. Rarest of all, though, was the spiraled tusk of that elusive arctic whale, the narwhal. Christened the "unicorn of the sea" by some, the male of the species sports a slender spearlike tusk (technically a tooth) that can approach nine feet in length. Though no longer believed to possess magical powers, these tusks were nonetheless considered very special raw material by the few scrimshanders lucky enough to acquire one of them.

Supplementing these basic materials were woods like pine and cedar, available on shipboard, and a wide range of mahoganies and other tropical woods found at far-flung ports of call. Tortoiseshell and horn occasionally made their way into scrimshaw articles as well. The iridescent quality of mother-of-pearl, found in abalone and other mollusks, often served as inlay to highlight design details. Moreover, coconut shells, shark vertebrae, and metals like pewter and silver were employed in certain instances.

. . . and Methods

Our scrimshander did not pick up a raw tooth and immediately begin engraving, no matter how skilled an artist he was. First the ridged tooth had to be prepared, and the sooner the better, as the relatively soft material hardened with exposure to air. Soaking in hot brine was said to keep teeth fairly soft if immediate preparation was impossible. A file or sharp knife, followed by an abrasive like sandpaper, sharkskin, or pumice, could normally transform the tooth into a smooth, workable medium. If intended to stand upright, the tooth's jagged base was usually sawed off square.

Once satisfied with the surface, the scrimshander would plan the design, perhaps sketching on the tooth in pencil, and then begin his engraving using a jackknife, sail needle, awl, file, or any combination of these and other available tools [7]. Melville noted in *Moby-Dick* that some of the more dedicated artists

owned "little boxes of dentistical-looking implements" for detail work.[25]

An artist might find his inspiration in real-life events and objects; in printed illustrations from various sources; or from his own fertile imagination. These scenes or concepts were then tooled onto the tooth.

An interesting variation to freehand design was the so-called "pin-prick" method, whereby a printed illustration would be attached directly to the tooth and pricks with a sail needle or like instrument would delineate the key outlines of the pattern. The

7. Scrimshanders used a variety of implements, some homemade. Clockwise from top: awl with whalebone handle, 3 3/8 in. (8.5 cm.); sail needle stylus with whalebone handle, 6 3/4 in. (17.1 cm.); jackknife, 6 5/16 in. (16.0 cm.); and saw with whalebone frame, 5 13/16 in. (13.2 cm.). *Sources:* Dr. Charles K. Stillman, 36.111; Anonymous, 70.121; Paul Schoonman, 49.326; Charles E. White, 39.2020

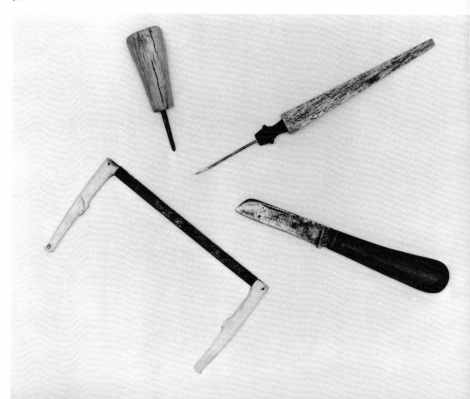

8. A detail of "pin-prick" work on a sperm whale tooth.
Source: Charles E. White, 39.1721

illustration was then removed and a strategy of "connect the dots" would ensue, transferring the original design to the ivory surface [8]. Extra detail could be added or not, at the whim of the scrimshander.

Once satisfied with the engraving work, the sailor's next step was to bring out the design by "inking" the piece with whatever material was at hand: india ink, soot or charcoal from the tryworks, lampblack, or similar coatings produced black, the most popular effect; sepia coloring could be achieved using tobacco juice or even rust; and copper oxide or "patina" was occasionally used for greens. Besides whatever inks might be available, there were some rather exotic hues traditionally used by Asian and Pacific peoples that might also find their way on board during a voyage.[26] Once the excess surface coloring was wiped off, the engraved design stood out boldly against the white ivory.

Some scrimshanders sought the "antique" look by staining the teeth with tea or tobacco juice, though most went directly on to the final step and buffed the piece to a high gloss. While a bit of oil, sailmaker's wax,[27] or ashes occasionally supplemented a soft cloth and the palm of the hand, it was that liberal dose of elbow grease which usually lent the tooth its sheen.

Though sailors rarely carved teeth in relief as in the Oriental tradition, whale ivory was often used in the fabrication of other items, notably cane handles, jagging wheels, and winding swifts. Rarely was a lathe available for widespread use, so that much of the "turned" work is actually the result of expertise with saw and file. Many of the decorative grooves or scribings on turned pieces of ivory and bone were filled with hard, colored sealing wax, predominantly red, instead of ink.

Pieces of whalebone, usually panbone from the sperm whale, could be handled with the same few tools as ivory, though often very flat sections were cut out for use as decorative plaques on which detailed vessel portraits or elaborate whaling panoramas were depicted. When shaved thin and steamed this same bone could be bent for use in oval or circular boxes and other articles.[28] As with ivory, whalebone is stronger and less brittle when it is fresh, hence its periodic use in rugged shipboard gear like blocks, fids, and belaying pins.

Walrus ivory could be handled in much the same manner as whale teeth, though the smoother tusks required a bit less surface preparation before engraving. In addition to providing the potential for a decorative masterpiece, the tusk was admirably suited for conversion into winding swift shafts, candlesticks, long jagging wheels, and other implements requiring ivory of considerable length and straightness.

The thousands of pounds of baleen reaped in the processing of bowhead and right whales provided an unlimited supply of material for the ambitious scrimshander. With access to baleen pieces up to twelve feet in length at times, the sky was the limit for a resourceful whaleman. One decorated strip [26] in the Museum's collection measures nearly seven feet in height. Once cleaned, dried, and cut to workable size the baleen could be engraved like ivory or bone, sometimes with a white powder rubbed into the design for contrast.[29] When heated or steamed, this material could be bent much like panbone. In addition, baleen was often used as decorative inlay in larger bone or ivory items. Horn too was used, and it is often difficult to differentiate between these two substances in a given object.

Though wood was employed extensively in the structure of some scrimshaw items, it is most usually found in a secondary role, that of providing visual and textural contrast. More often than not materials like mother-of-pearl, horn, tortoiseshell, and metal contributed purely aesthetic qualities to the final product.

Chapter 2 *The Collection: A Half Century of Growth*

In the Beginning . . .

IT BEGAN as a trickle, the Museum's collection; and before long the trickle became a flood as hundreds of items, singly and in groups, came to the fledgling Marine Historical Association during its first years of existence, 1929-1938. The collecting policy was very broad, or at least loosely defined, by today's standards. Anything remotely connected with the sea was gratefully accepted by Messrs. Cutler, Bradley, Stillman [9], and their band of early supporters.

Though the first item donated to the Museum was a book, it was not long, 1931 to be exact, before scrimshaw first entered the collection in the form of a corset busk. A gift of Mrs. Harriet Greenman Stillman, this busk, the 206th artifact acquired by the Mystic museum, presaged the flood of scrimshaw that would on occasion virtually inundate Carl Cutler's tiny curatorial staff in the coming years.

Over the next half dozen years Mrs. Stillman, along with her son, Dr. Charles K. Stillman, one of the Association's three founders, purchased various scrimshaw items for Mystic's growing collection.

The Museum's holdings of models, paintings, photographs, watercraft, etc., developed steadily during the decades of the 1930s and 1940s. But for the scrimshaw collection the ten years or so beginning in 1939 were to become a period of unprecedented growth.

An Incredible Decade

It all began with a bank, believe it or not. Over a period of many years New London's Mariners Savings Bank had built up a fine collection of whaling material, including prints, paintings, whaling gear and, of course, scrimshaw. This collection was displayed in the bank's State Street office and served, in effect, as a small whaling museum.

In the summer of 1939 the Mariners Savings Bank consolidated with the larger Savings Bank of New London. One victim of the merger was the old Mariners Bank facility, which was soon closed, leaving the fine whaling collection homeless.[1]

Dame Fortune smiled on the Marine Historical Association as the bank's trustees decided that this collection should come on loan to Mystic, in spite of the interest expressed by New London's own Lyman Allyn Museum and New London County Historical Society. Of the hundreds of items in the bank's collection there were nearly fifty examples of scrimshaw, including teeth, tusks, canes, busks, and fids. A newly reconditioned Stillman Building soon housed the collection.

Even before the dust had settled on the Savings Bank of New London scrimshaw, yet another collection appeared on the horizon. Charles E. White, since 1930 President of the Savings Bank of New London, had been instrumental in bringing the bank's whaling collection to Mystic. But White, a trustee of the young Marine Historical Association, was also a scrimshaw

9. The Museum's three founders, Carl C. Cutler, Edward E. Bradley, and Dr. Charles K. Stillman, as they appeared in the early 1930s. *Source:* Seaport Photo Archives

collector of some forty or fifty years standing. Beginning with pieces inherited from his father, New London shipmaster and whaling captain Edwin W. White, Charles White had built up a collection of nearly three hundred pieces. Many were gifts from descendants of other New London whaling families.[2] Mystic's curator, Carl Cutler, was nearly beside himself with joy when he heard of Charles White's intention to loan the collection to the Museum. White made this material an outright gift early in 1940. Virtually overnight Mystic's scrimshaw collection became one of the finest anywhere.

Almost mercifully for the hard-pressed curatorial staff, scrim-shaw acquisitions slowed to a more manageable pace; that is, until there arrived on the scene one Gerald Fox, a collector *par excellence* from Massachusetts. During the 1920s and 1930s Fox had gathered an impressive collection of scrimshaw, manuscript material, lighting devices, and other items. Hundreds of pieces from his collection, including nearly two hundred examples of scrimshaw, arrived early in 1942 as a loan exhibit. Most, including pieces credited to the hands of scrimshanders Fred Smith and Josiah Robinson, were later purchased by the Museum through the generosity of trustee Harold H. Kynett.

The Fox collection typified the problems of adequately researching and cataloging sizable collections built up over many years. Trying to make some headway in the task of developing documentation for the hundreds of Fox collection items, the staff asked the collector for any information he had about each piece, especially its history or provenance. Fox's colorful reply that he had "gathered the collection while still a carefree, curly-headed lad rolling a hoop through God's free acres" dashed most hopes of creating a usable body of research data.[3] Nonetheless, the Fox collection remains one of the Museum's finest in terms of quality; and bit by bit more is learned about many of its individual scrimshaw pieces.

As early as 1940 Mrs. Raynham Townshend of New Haven had expressed an interest in Mystic's collection of scrimshaw. Carl Cutler was invited to the Elm City to view the many examples of this work collected by Mrs. Townshend's late husband, Dr. Raynham Townshend. A son of Captain Charles H. Townshend, noted packet and steamship commander, Dr. Townshend had gathered a group of well over one hundred pieces of scrimshaw. Early in 1948 the collection arrived at Mystic, a gift of Mrs. Townshend.

But the year 1948 was not even half over when yet another private collection of scrimshaw, that of the late Charles H. Martin, came, the gift of Mrs. Martin. A total of over 165 examples of this mariner's art had thus arrived by mid-summer, broadening both the scope and depth of the Museum's scrimshaw collection.

Complementing these several sizable acquisitions was a steady influx of additional material from many sources. Individual donations from far and wide helped boost Mystic's collection to well over seven hundred pieces by the end of these hectic ten years, 1939-1949.

A Rediscovered Art

Almost as abruptly as it had started, the wave of large scrimshaw acquisitions ceased about 1950. Whether this marked the twilight of one generation of collectors is uncertain; but after this the Seaport, as we now styled ourselves, relied increasingly on the continued donations of individual pieces, as well as on small museum purchases.

During the decade of the 1950s scrimshaw was beginning to emerge from the shadows and assume an identity all its own. The popular image of scrimshaw as something archaic, a curiosity, and only incidental to the major threads of our maritime past, was slowly changing. In time it was seen and appreciated, by more than just a handful of collectors and museums, for what it really was—and is—a slice of history; a reflection not simply of the whaling industry, but of America's maritime achievements, which played such a significant role in the nation's early development.

It is curious to speculate about just what effect popular films like the 1956 remake of *Moby Dick* had on the public's appreciation of our maritime past. Certainly the Disney-inspired "Davy Crockett" phenomenon raised, if indirectly, the historical consciousness of the American public in the 1950s, a process that, nurtured by the Bicentennial celebration and *Roots* in the 1970s, continues to this day.

For scrimshaw the positive trend continued unabated into the 1960s, no doubt boosted by John Kennedy's much-publicized collection. New private collections were being formed, and the Seaport found itself receiving fewer and fewer donations of this material.

With the advent of the 1970s scrimshaw basked in the widening popularity seemingly enjoyed by all forms of folk art. A "*Susan*'s tooth" became the *ne plus ultra* of scrimshaw collecting. Indeed, several record auction prices were set by Frederick Myrick's 150-year-old handiwork.

The Collection: Now and Tomorrow

In the face of high prices and stiff competition for marine items among museums, collectors, and investors, the Seaport rethought its collecting philosophy. The loose policy of seeking anything related to the sea was revised in the light of rising costs, shortages of suitable exhibit and storage space, and a desire to concentrate more on the nineteenth-century American maritime experience. The goal of the Museum was now to refine the collection in general.

As applied to scrimshaw, this entailed selected purchases of items to flesh out our holdings. Increased emphasis was placed on the aesthetic quality of a piece, as well as on an item's historical significance, most especially its connection with a specific vessel or individual.

Though most scrimshaw pieces remain the work of anonymous hands, ongoing historical research has identified more and more scrimshanders: men like Edward Burdett of Nantucket, T. L. Albro of Newport, Rhode Island, Benjamin W. Bradford of Bristol, Rhode Island, and Captain Frederick H. Smith of New Bedford. It seems likely that as time goes on this trend will continue and with it the Museum's active collection of individual scrimshaw examples.

More than half a century has passed since that first scrimshaw busk entred the Museum, and the years have seen growth not only in the size and variety of our scrimshaw collection, but also in our understanding and appreciation of this most creative of nautical arts.

Chapter 3 *Decorative Scrimshaw*

THE Museum's many scrimshaw items can be categorized in any number of ways, including style, technique, material, intended use, and artistic quality. The most basic distinction, though, is implied in the brief definition of scrimshaw in Chapter 1: Scrimshaw includes decorative carving or engraving on certain materials, and construction of useful handmade items using the same basic substances. Scrimshaw pieces, then, can be purely decorative or utilitarian in nature, though many of the latter items are also elaborately ornamented. Decorative items are intended to be viewed, while utilitarian items are designed for specific uses.

The most popular medium for decorative scrimshaw is the sperm whale tooth, followed in frequency by slabs of flat pan-bone, the impressive walrus tusk, and pieces of baleen. The large surface areas of these materials lend themselves to the graphic treatments so popular among nineteenth-century scrimshanders. Detailed ship portraits, panoramic whaling scenes, classic naval engagements, elaborate human portraits, these and many other motifs appear on decorative scrimshaw in the collection. But upon what sources did the scrimshander draw for inspiration?

One must not underestimate the imagination of the whaleman when considering the wealth of decorative scrimshaw produced. Many of the crewmen were young and animated characters, determined to escape the seeming drudgery of farm or small town by shipping aboard a vessel. Whaling voyages were usually not the lucrative, lively ventures described by the advertising posters or deceitful shoreside recruiters. But it normally took more than one voyage to dull or extinguish youthful spirit and creativity. Imagination, and memory too, fueled by exotic sights, unusual events, or homesickness, played an important creative role for the scrimshander. Imagination and memory were especially important in the eighteenth and early nineteenth centuries, before the advent of mass-produced illustrative materials such as prints reduced the scrimshander's dependence on these mental powers alone.

With the development of popular, inexpensive prints, notably lithographs, during the second quarter of the nineteenth century, a new range of visual material was available to the artist. Famous people and events, domestic scenes, landscapes, ship portraits—these and many other subjects could be transferred to bone and ivory, in whole or in part, with sometimes startling accuracy.

Book, newspaper, and magazine illustrations were yet another source of imagery to be tapped. Battle scenes, portraits of people in the news or characters from literature and history, notable landmarks, and women's fashions represent some of the more popular illustrated subjects borrowed by the shipbound artist. Toward the end of the nineteenth century the availability of photographs provided yet another avenue of visual inspiration, one that continues to be used today by contemporary practitioners.

Elaborate border designs or geometric patterns appearing on engraved pieces sometimes found their origin in such everyday items as decorated tinware, or even cigar boxes. Commercially available stencil patterns could also supply some ideas,[1] though the scrimshander would almost certainly have to reduce the scale of the designs.

Normally, it is almost impossible to identify the exact illustration used by a scrimshander in creating a particular decorative piece. The Museum, however, is fortunate to have a number of items for which a specific image model can be positively identified. These pieces will be considered individually, according to the particular subject matter portrayed.

Let's examine one at a time, then, those major topics and decorative motifs popular with many scrimshanders.

Whales

One of the earliest subjects to occupy the whaleman-artist's attention was the whale itself. This creature, after all, was a central figure in the hunt, the source of the scrimshander's livelihood as well as his raw materials. It was only natural that this giant should find its way into the art of scrimshaw.

The research that has been done so far seems to discount the idea that there might have been any spiritual association with the whale on the part of the whaleman.[2] The whale was prey, a potential source of wealth, to be harvested like any crop ashore. The scrimshander's depiction of the animal was not so much calculated to capture its spirit or essence, a practice in some native cultures, as to illustrate its size and appearance. This was

10. The tooth at left documents the capture of a sperm whale giant in 1884, 5 in. (12.7 cm.). At right, a bit of artistic license places a sperm whale atop the waves, 6³/₈ in. (16.2 cm.). *Sources:* Charles E. White, 39.1779; Mrs. Raynham Townshend, 47.1361

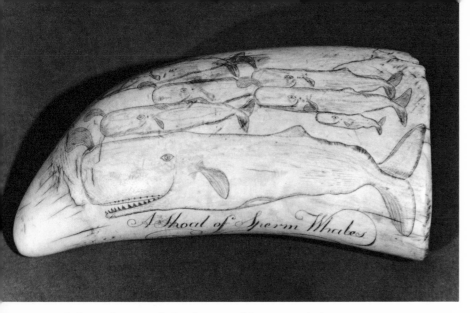

11. Whales and more whales decorate this sperm whale tooth, dated "Dec^br 1818," 7 1/8 in. (18.1 cm.).
Source: Museum purchase, 46.1480

12. Matched pair of teeth engraved aboard the New London whaler *Neptune,* 1849, 5 1/2 in. (14.0 cm.).
Source: Charles E. White, 39.1734, 39.1729

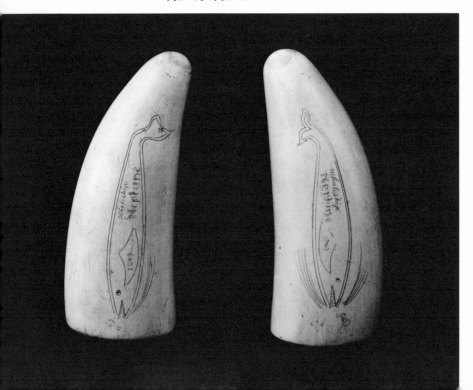

especially true in the case of the large sperm whale with its impressive head and teeth.

The sperm whale is the species most often represented in decorative scrimshaw. For decades it was the preferred quarry of American whalemen due to its high-quality oil. Its reputation as a fighter enhanced the value of its teeth as trophies of sorts.[3] And what better whale to illustrate than the species from which the tooth actually came?

A number of sperm whale teeth in the Museum's collection show this leviathan spouting while actually *sitting* atop the waves, an achievement that eluded Moby Dick even on his best day. One of the more elaborate of these pieces [10] is quite heavily engraved, and inked in both red and black for added effect.

A documentary piece is a whale tooth [10] that is decorated with a finely engraved profile of a sperm whale. Dated "May 22 1884," it records that this whale yielded a whopping "100 BBLS." of oil, a feat that no doubt pleased our unknown scrimshander and his crewmates. It is ironic, though, to see such a large sperm whale taken late in the century when baleen whales like the right and bowhead were the preferred catch. Had this whale been taken fifty years earlier it would have been an even greater cause for shipboard rejoicing.

A comparison of the engraving work on this well-executed piece with that on the previous whale tooth suggests that this scrimshander used an illustration as a model. The fine proportions of the whale's body were difficult to capture through simply viewing the creature in the water. The cutting-in process so obliterated the whale's true form that even close observation might not provide sufficient help for the artist. A very similar engraving appears in G. Brown Goode's *The Fisheries and Fishery Industries of the United States,* published in 1884, the same year the whale was taken.

For a whimsical treatment of the normally fearsome-looking sperm whale it's hard to beat the tooth [11] engraved with "A Shoal of Sperm Whales." A group of seven whales, including a calf, are pictured cruising in close formation. To a one they wear the most pleasant smiles; indeed, the appearance of prominent teeth in the largest individual can only be interpreted as a good-natured grin. Of all our teeth this one comes closest, perhaps, to an anthropomorphic treatment of the creature. The scrimshander has worked some very human-like qualities into his engraved whales, to the point that they are reminiscent of a family out for a Sunday stroll. Our talented but unidentified artist notes on the reverse that this is indeed "A Sperm Whale's Tooth"; and the inscription "Dec^br 1818" makes it one of the earliest dated pieces in the Museum collection.

An interesting matched pair of teeth [12] sports stylized whales, each marked "Whaleship Neptune 1849." The *Neptune,* a 285-ton whaler from nearby New London, Connecticut, commanded by Henry Holt, was operating in the Indian Ocean at the time the teeth were engraved. The vessel returned home early in 1850, having been at sea about 2½ years. If accounts of the ship's catch are any indication, these teeth are from one of the very few sperm whales taken on the voyage.

Several whale teeth are actually carved in the shape of whales, an exception to the usual technique of simply engraving whales on the surface of the ivory. One specimen [13] admittedly looks more fishlike, but its incised verse leaves no doubt as to the creature's identity:

> Remember –
> Never is heart more brave and free
> Than he who hunts the whale at sea.

A small engraved sperm whale complements the brief rhyme on this piece, which could easily have been intended as a gift for a

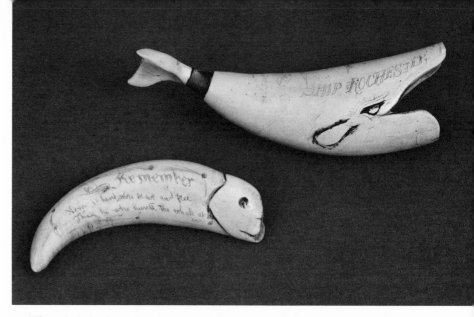

13. The whale in three dimensions. Above, a masterfully carved souvenir of the whaler *Rochester,* 6¼ in (15.9 cm.). Below, a whaleman's verse on a sculpted tooth, 4½ in. (11.5 cm.). *Sources:* Charles E. White, 39.1802; Mrs. Raynham Townshend, 47.1381

wife or sweetheart. Unfortunately the identity of our shipboard artist-poet remains a mystery.

A remarkable tooth [13] was carved by a crewman aboard the *Rochester* in 1842. There is no mistaking the identity of this, a sperm whale whose gaping mouth is formed by the carved butt end of the tooth. Carved whale ivory flukes are attached to the tip of the tooth by a band of baleen or horn. The top of the piece is marked "SHIP ROCHESTER" and records that vessel's visits to the Seychelle Islands in the Indian Ocean, Rarotonga in the Cook Islands northeast of New Zealand, Peru, and Valparaiso, Chile. This tooth was previously believed to be American, but apparently there was no U.S. whaler by this name active in 1842. Research indicates, however, that the London firm of Hill & Co. had a 393-ton whaler *Rochester* in the South Pacific at this time;[4] and this unusual tooth is quite possibly the inspired handiwork of one of her crew. This case, then, serves to illustrate the difficulty of determining the national origin of many scrimshaw items.

Whaling

Whaling attracted thousands of ambitious young men hoping to strike it rich through a successful voyage. While only a relatively small percentage of these individuals benefited financially from whaling, they all shared an identity as whalemen. A good deal of romantic nonsense obscured the character of the whaleman, especially during the late nineteenth and early twentieth centuries when American whaling was fast becoming little more than a memory. This "Yo Heave Ho!" school of American whaling history, as it is sometimes jokingly referred to, with its popular image of the heroic whaleman, contrasts sharply with our own views of the man-whale relationship.

Undoubtedly there was a certain glory accorded the whaleman, especially during the forty or so years preceding the Civil War, when the Yankee fleet, manned largely by Americans, roamed the oceans at will, supplying commodities commonly used in everyday life. Ashore, the whaleman who had successfully harpooned a whale might wear as a badge a small whalebone replica of a harpooner's peg in his hat. This peg, used to control the harpoon line as it played out of the whaleboat's bow, became in miniature a mark of distinction widely recognized in whaling ports.[5]

Grumble as they might over the shortcomings of whaling life, returning whalemen could nonetheless take pride in having endured the many dangers and privations incident to the voyage. Those moments of special excitement or glory were all

14. Classic whaling scenes on sperm whale teeth. Note the overturned whaleboat on the first tooth, 6⅛ in. (15.5 cm.). A whaleboat's sailing rig is clearly illustrated on the companion tooth, 6¼ in. (15.9 cm.). *Sources:* Harold H. Kynett, 55.462; Mrs. James H. Stivers, 40.115

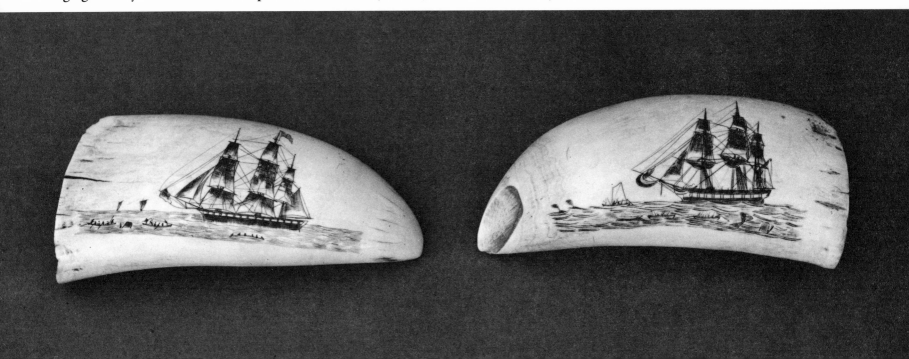

theirs to relate, and many of these episodes were memorialized on bone and ivory. It comes as no surprise, then, that the activity of whaling became an extremely popular subject for the whaleman-artist. This appears to have been especially true in the first third of the nineteenth century, before mass-produced illustrations offered the scrimshander alternative subject material.

That portion of the voyage actually devoted to pursuing and capturing whales was quite small, yet this was the aspect which proved so popular to many scrimshanders. The interminable hours of searching the horizon for whales and the exhausting, filthy task of cutting in whales and processing the blubber on deck were not particularly popular scrimshaw subjects. Most cutting-in scenes, in fact, are but distant views, and even here there is often more exciting whaling activity developing in the foreground. The scrimshander would much rather dwell on those infrequent moments of excitement, and in doing so ease the burden caused by long periods of inactivity.

It is not surprising that the sperm whale hunt appears so often on scrimshaw items, especially teeth and panbone. In addition to its obvious economic importance to the whaleman, the hunted sperm whale could also generate quite a bit of excitement—and frequently did. At the hands of a scrimshander such excitement could become visual pandemonium as tiny whaleboats pursued the elusive creatures across expanses of bone and ivory.

Two teeth [14] in the collection serve to introduce us to whaling through the eyes of the scrimshander. The first of these pieces includes many of the elements common to whaling scenes: a solitary whaleship under reduced sail in the distance; sperm whales depicted in such varied attitudes as "sounding" or diving, surfacing, cruising along the surface, and spouting; and one or more small whaleboats engaged in pursuit or attack.

Harpoons are being thrown at two of the whales from the boats in the foreground. An interesting addition is the presence of a whaleboat under sail, pursuing the pair of whales marked by the spouts to the left.

The second piece uses much the same composition, though the quality of the engraving is better. Of special interest here is the capsized whaleboat just below the whaleship, probably the result of a close encounter with an intended victim. The boat's six-man crew can be seen clinging to the overturned craft, awaiting rescue by their shipmates.

A more vivid rendering of what could happen when the hunter became the hunted is provided on yet another sperm whale tooth [15]. Our scrimshander has captured on ivory the image of a wounded sperm whale neatly bisecting a twenty-five-foot whaleboat and, presumably, its crew. The harpoons or "irons" in the whale's flank no doubt explain the creature's

15. One whale's revenge as seen by a whaleman, 5½ in. (14.0 cm.). *Source:* Charles E. White, 39.1738

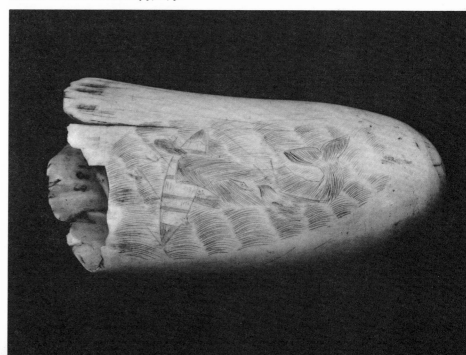

exasperation. Red ink is used to simulate the whale's oozing lifeblood, leaving little doubt as to the outcome of the contest.

The unknown engraver of another tooth [16], though perhaps less practiced than some, provides one of our closer views of the whaleman's seaborne attack. Riding on a green sea, two whaleboats, their crews uniformly attired in broadbrimmed hats, have each attacked a sperm whale. One victim has just sounded, and the line is playing out of the boat's bow as the panicked animal heads for deep water trying to escape. In the meantime the harpooner in the boat to the left is preparing to dart a second iron into his surfaced prey. Incidentally, the scene wraps around the tooth, revealing a whaleship and two additional whaleboats in the water.

A series of panbone plaques neatly illustrates whalebone's potential as a scrimshander's "canvas." One boldly engraved piece [17] shows four sperm whales harpooned simultaneously

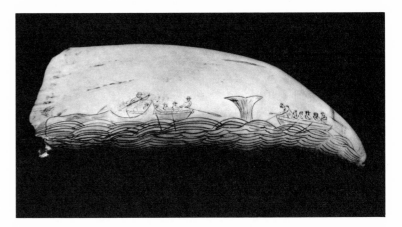

16. A closeup of the whalehunt as depicted on a tooth, 6⅛ in. (15.5 cm.). *Source:* Charles E. White, 39.1793

from four different whaleboats. Each crew has shipped oars as if preparing for a "Nantucket sleigh ride," that is, a wild tow ride behind a harpooned whale. Just noticeable in the extreme lower center is the dead whale marked by a "waif," a flag and pole planted in the carcass that served to identify both the location and ownership of the whale if immediate recovery was impossible. The lookout visible up the foremast of the whaling bark is pointing to four more whales spouting at the right of the scene—a whaling bonanza indeed! This 5¾ by 8⅞ inch piece is further distinguished by crosshatched border decoration.

The sperm whale fishery is once again the topic of an engraved panbone slab [18]. A nicely detailed whaleship hugs the right edge, while the rest of the 15½-inch-long scene is given over to particulars of the hunt. The whaleboats are well portrayed, as is the clothing of the crew in the nearest whaleboat. Again, red coloring simulates blood from the stricken whales. The appearance of four irregularly spaced holes in the piece, including one that unfortunately obliterates one of the graceful

17. "Greasy Luck" is the theme of this unsigned panbone plaque, 5¾ x 8⅞ in. (14.6 x 22.5 cm.). *Source:* Harold H. Kynett, 55.1199

corner fan designs, suggests that the plaque has been mounted in several different ways over the years.

Sperm whales preferred fairly temperate waters, drawing many whaleships to tropical and equatorial seas. Such a locale provides the setting for a truly spectacular piece of decorative scrimshaw [Cover; see color plate opp. p. 80]. The now familiar whaling action is impressive enough: two sailing whaleboats attacking a group of whales, with a third boat dangerously close to a whale in its violent death throes. But what sets this panbone scene apart is the obvious effort taken in setting the entire scene. A pair of whaling barks, one offshore and another lying in a sheltered bay, explains the presence of the hunters. The lush green vegetation of the two islands, one of which is also an active volcano with flowing lava, contrasts vividly with the dark texture of the surrounding waters. At least six colors are used in highlighting the exquisite engraving work of our unknown artist, who manages to epitomize the popular image of the

18. A graceful whaling panorama executed on panbone, 4⅝ x 15½ in. (11.8 x 39.4 cm.). *Source:* Museum purchase, 52.39

19. Life and death in the sperm whale fishery as depicted on panbone by an unknown scrimshander, 4³/₄ x 9³/₄ in. (12.1 x 24.7 cm.). *Source:* Mrs. Alexander O. Vietor, 81.64.17

South Seas in an area measuring 4³/₈ by 8³/₈ inches. This is truly work of the highest order.

A somewhat less inviting scene is depicted on another pan-bone plaque [19]. Unlike the preceding scene, the land visible in the background is uniformly brown and barren of growth. The floating chaos prevailing in the foreground shows how effective a sperm whale counterattack could be. Although the large whale in the foreground is *in extremis* as a killing lance is thrust into its vitals, and a waif marks a previous kill in the distance, the creatures are nevertheless exacting a toll of their own. A whaleboat has just been snapped in two by an enraged whale, and its crew and gear can be seen raining down on the water. The boat to the left has apparently been stove in and is taking water as one of her crew bails furiously to keep the craft afloat. This stalemate is broken, however, by the appearance of a trio of sailing whaleboats in the distance, each towing a dead

· 40 ·

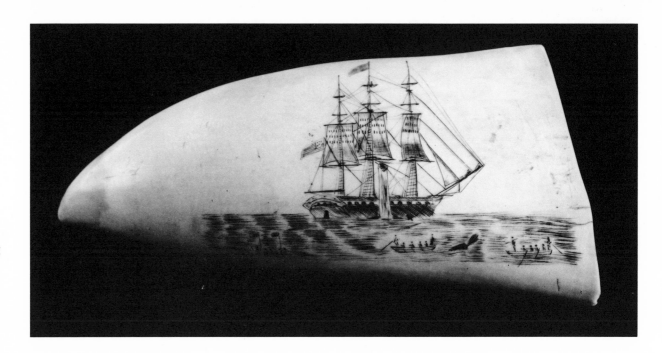

20. Cutting in a whale, showing the large "blanket piece" of blubber being hoisted aloft, 6¾ in. (17.2 cm.). *Source:* Museum purchase, 52.42

whale. These hunters appear to have had an easier time of it as they head home, probably to the whaler partly visible at the right edge. Twin mounting holes pierce the sawtooth border of this 4¾ by 9¾ inch slab.

Once the kill was made the whale would be towed back to the vessel for the trying-out process, which rendered blubber into whale oil. As mentioned, most scrimshaw views of this procedure are from a distance, the large suspended strip of blubber called a "blanket piece" clearly visible amidships. American whaling vessels normally cut in a whale on the right or starboard side, so this is almost always the view depicted by the scrimshander. Only after the blubber was further cut into smaller pieces aboard ship was it placed in the iron try-pots for rendering. Wisps of smoke from the tryworks, located amidships, are occasionally visible on engraved scenes.

One tooth [20] presents a very clear view of the cutting-in operation, while whaling action continues in the foreground. There is a marked similarity of style to the engraving work found on a previously illustrated tooth [14]. Similar scenes appear on several other teeth in the Seaport collection.

The 6 by 13½ inch flat surface of a panbone piece [21] is well utilized to catalog various whaling activities. But in this instance attention is drawn first to the vivid cutting-in scene, which shows what appears to be a right whale being stripped of its thick coat of blubber. The large iron "blubber hook" is visible, pierced through the hanging blanket piece near the top.

Though less common than teeth or panbone, walrus tusks were occasionally employed in recording whaling events. Perhaps the scrimshander was able to acquire them directly from Eskimos in the North Pacific area, or maybe he obtained them by purchase or barter from other whalemen. Whatever the

21. Heavily stylized water distinguishes this panbone whaling scene, which features a fine cutting-in view, 6 x 13½ in. (15.2 x 34.3 cm.). *Source:* Charles E. White, 39.1962

method of procurement, tusks did find their way aboard whaleships, to undergo the same transformation as whale teeth.

Captain Frederick Vincent commanded the 321-ton New Bedford whaleship *Swift* on a 3½-year voyage to the Pacific during the years 1853 through 1856. On that voyage an unknown crewman utilized a twenty-one-inch-long walrus tusk [22] to create what he called a "RECORD—WHALESHIP SWIFT—NEW BEDFORD—1855." The front of the tusk is decorated with a scene of the *Swift* cutting in a whale, with the blanket piece so labeled in capital letters. An attack on a large sperm whale is also pictured on this side along with the motto "Sperm as I live" and the notation "In the Pacific Ocean West of New Zeland."

The so-called "RECORD" is engraved on the reverse and lists as well as graphically depicts three sperm whales that escaped and, more important, eight that did not. The first of these, taken

· 42 ·

10 January 1854 off the "Gallapagoes," yielded ninety-one barrels of oil. Others were taken at places like "French Rock," a tiny mid-ocean rockpile in the rich whaling grounds north of New Zealand, and "Off Apia June 4 1855." The "Navigator Islands" noted on the front refer to what is now Samoa, of which Apia is a leading port. As the last two recorded kills occurred off these islands, it is probable that the tusk was engraved in this area in mid-1855.

Though the tally of eight whales totaling over 650 barrels of oil is impressive, our scrimshander would have done well to stock several more tusks, as the *Swift's* final eighteen months' activity netted enough whales to yield another 1500 barrels of oil. "Sperm as I live" certainly proved more than an idle boast for this unknown artist and his shipmates.

A splendid matched pair of walrus tusks were engraved in 1842 aboard the Nantucket whaleship *Spartan,* David Coffin master. The 334-ton vessel was almost three years out on a Pacific voyage when our scrimshander began his off-duty project. Decorating one tusk [22] is a scene showing a whaleboat under sail, a dead whale marked with a waif, and a whaleship in the distance. To the right of the whale is the legend "Ship Spartan of NANTUCKET/OFF SHORE GROUNDS/July 7 1842." Over three weeks later this piece's mate was engraved "Ship Spartan of NANTUCKET/OFF SHORE GROUNDS/August 1st 1842." A neatly etched spouting whale and a view of the *Spartan* cutting in a whale complete the scenario begun on the first tusk.

It is rare enough to find scrimshaw items from clearly identified vessels, but when both vessel and scrimshander are known

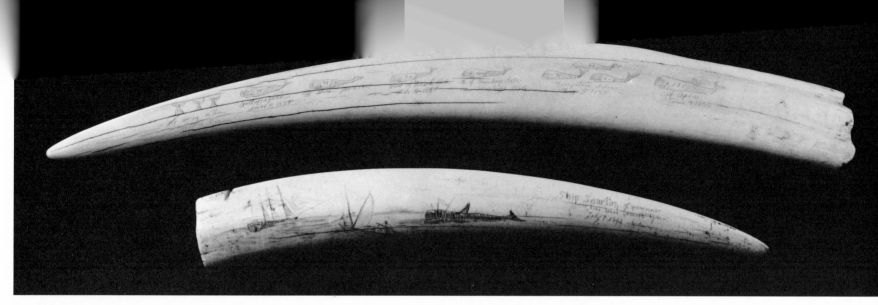

22. Walrus tusks could also document whaling activity. Above, a whaling tally for the ship *Swift* in 1855, 21¼ in. (54.0 cm.). Below, one of a pair of tusks engraved aboard the whaleship *Spartan* in 1842, 13⅞ in. (35.3 cm.).
Sources: Charles E. White, 39.1873; Mrs. Raynham Townshend, 47.1347

a piece acquires additional historical significance. Such is the case with a number of the Museum's whaling-oriented decorative scrimshaw objects: for example, a finely engraved tooth [23] showing a broadside view of the 403-ton whaleship *Friends,* inscribed "Friends of New London Chaseing Whales" on the front, and bearing a detailed portrait of the whaleship "Wm Tell of New York a Cutting" on the reverse [24]. The tooth is clearly marked "Engraved by Edward Burdett," a whaleman believed to have been born on Nantucket in October 1805.[6] Burdett's style is direct yet quite detailed, especially in its treatment of the vessels. The engraving work is uniformly deep and undoubtedly stood out in bold relief when newly inked. Faintly etched in the sky above the *Friends* is the word "CARVE," suggesting perhaps that Burdett planned to include clouds, the sun, or even more birds in the scene. Burdett, who served aboard the *William Tell,* possibly produced the tooth in the mid-

1840s when both of these vessels were active in the same North Pacific waters. The history of the *William Tell* prior to 1843 is too vague for us to suggest an earlier date for the tooth. The fact of the Nantucketer's service aboard the *William Tell* is verified by a remarkably similar tooth [24] in a private collection that illustrates the same two whaleships and notes "ENGRAVED BY EDWARD BURDETT, OF NANTUCKET ON BOARD OF THE/ WM TELL." Other examples of Burdett's work, with its distinctive vinework border and stylized water, can be found in the collections of the Peabody Museum of Salem, Massachusetts, and the Kendall Whaling Museum in Sharon, Massachusetts.

Samuel Huggins, Jr., while shipping aboard the Nantucket whaleship *President* during a 2½-year voyage, whiled away some idle hours carving a truly documentary piece of scrimshaw. The 294-ton whaler, commanded by Captain Seth Cathcart, was almost two years into the voyage when whaleman

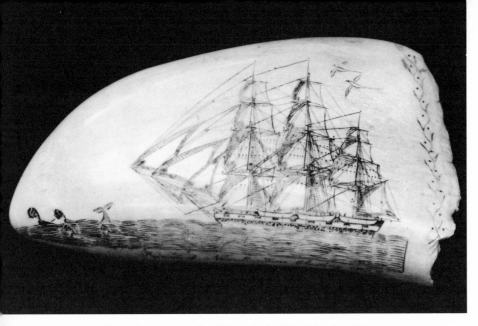

23. Edward Burdett's portrait of the whaleship *Friends* of New London, 5⅛ in. (13.0 cm.). *Source:* Harold H. Kynett, 56.172

24. Twin portraits of the whaleship *William Tell*. Above, Burdett's vessel cutting in a whale, 5⅛ in. (13.0 cm.). Below, a heavily inked view of the *William Tell* pursuing a sperm whale, 7¾ in. (19.7 cm.). *Sources:* Harold H. Kynett, 56.172; The Hollander Family Collection, 77.129

Huggins decided to log this entry on a sperm whale tooth:

SAMUEL.HUGGINS.JR.
SHIP.PRESIDENT.SOUTH.
PACIFIC.OCEAN.LATT
21 55S.LONG.175W.
OCT 20 1833.

On this date the *President* was about four hundred miles due south of the Fiji Islands, in the rich sperm whaling grounds so favored by the Americans. Huggins's work is characterized by clean, block lettering, a style aided by ruled lines lightly scribed on the tooth.

The English sperm whale fishery is ably represented in the work of one W. L. Roderick who, as a crew member aboard the bark *Adventure* in 1852, produced a number of fine scrimshaw teeth. The 237-ton British whaler, commanded by a Captain McCarty, was roaming the Atlantic about five hundred miles west of the Azores when she took a large sperm whale. One of Roderick's teeth [25] documents the kill:

The tooth of a Sperm
Whale Captured by Capt[n] M[c]Carty in the
North Atlantic Ocean Aug[st]
10th 1852 Latitude 39°11″ & Longitude
38°42″. and made 90. Blls
in the Barque Adventure

The tooth is signed "W. L. Roderick" at the left edge of the whaling scene, which plainly shows the *Adventure* with three whaleboats attacking a pair of sperm whales.

A companion tooth [25], apparently from the same whale, and listing the same date and nearly identical position, is similarly engraved. Here the *Adventure* is caught in the act of cutting in, while a pair of her whaleboats press the assault on several other sperm whales.

Roderick worked only one side of these teeth, leaving the reverse in its natural state. A deeply incised groove frames the scene on each piece, while the inscription appears at the tip. So fine is the incised lettering and so patiently detailed the whaling scenarios that one cannot help surmising that Roderick had some training as an artist or engraver. Whatever his background there is no doubt that some fine scrimshaw work was done aboard foreign whaleships.

Less common as a medium for purely decorative scrimshaw work is baleen. In the hands of a skilled artist, however, this material could produce exciting results. Consider the 6 foot 8 inch long strip [26] completely decorated on both sides with a wide variety of motifs, including whales, merchant and whaling vessels of different rigs, patriotic and geometric symbols, and several examples of flora. We are fortunate indeed that the artist decided to note the time and place of his labor, as well as his own identity. At the base of the baleen on one side is engraved the following:

JUNE.24th.1854
TAKEN BY BARQU[E]
SUPERIOR
E J D

The *Superior* of New Bedford, Charles L. Norton master, was a little over one year into a Pacific whaling voyage when she took the whale that provided this baleen. A study of her crew list indicates that an Ephraim J. Dodge shipped aboard her as a "green hand"; no doubt this was his first whaling voyage. His "lay" or share in the profits of the voyage was a paltry 1/175th, so without question he hoped for "greasy luck," the whaleman's equivalent of "good hunting." Alas, hunting was rather poor on this 1853-1856 voyage, only 794 barrels of sperm oil being stowed away in the hold. And it did not take many right whales to yield the 272 barrels of whale oil and 4200 pounds of baleen

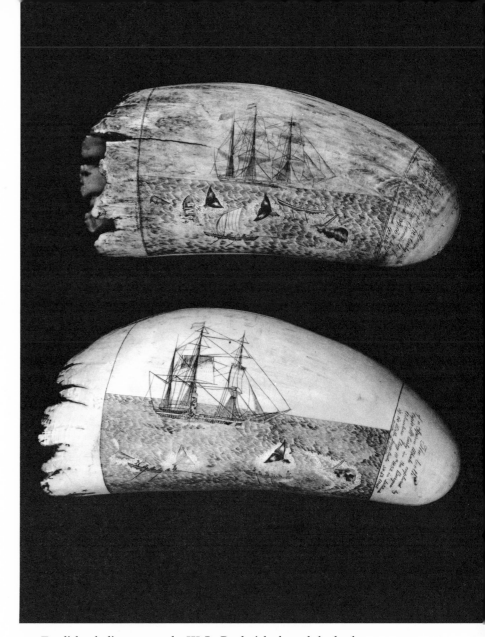

25. English whaling as seen by W. L. Roderick aboard the bark *Adventure*, 1852. Above, a stove boat and a dead whale, 7½ in. (19.0 cm.). Below, cutting in a whale, 8¼ in. (21.0 cm.). *Sources:* Museum purchase, 78.144; Harold H. Kynett, 56.173

26. An unusually large strip of baleen engraved by Ephraim J. Dodge in 1854, 6 ft. 8 in. (203.2 cm.). *Source:* C. L. Sibley, 61.1111

27. T. L. Albro depicted the whaleship *John Coggeshall* in South Pacific waters. "French Rock" is at the left, 8 3/8 in. (21.3 cm.). *Source:* Museum purchase, 81.40

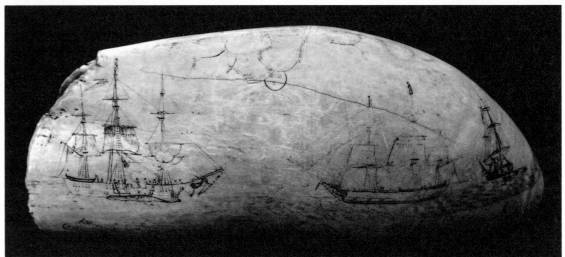

28. Reverse of Albro's *John Coggeshall* tooth, possibly illustrating three views of his ship, 8 3/8 in. (21.3 cm.). *Source:* Museum purchase, 81.40

29. Bottom edge of *Coggeshall* tooth featuring Albro's aquatic menagerie, 8 3/8 in. (21.3 cm.). *Source:* Museum purchase, 81.40

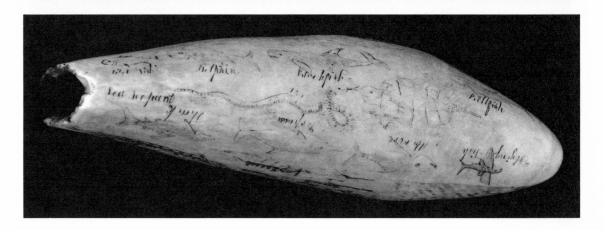

reported either. Make that 4198 pounds of baleen, as about 2 pounds of the material were tied up in Dodge's *magnum opus*.

So hunting was poor and time weighed heavily, two conditions bound to encourage Dodge and his shipmates to pursue diversions like scrimshaw. It can only be hoped that this indifferent showing prompted Dodge to take up other work upon his return home, or at least to ship aboard a different whaler. The *Superior*'s next voyage was to be her last, as the 276-ton vessel was attacked and burned by hostile natives in the Solomon Islands, September 1860. Only six of her crew escaped the massacre that ensued.

Several Rhode Island ports, notably Newport, claimed a share of the vast nineteenth-century American whaling fleet. The 338-ton ship *John Coggeshall* was one such vessel that called Newport home, from the time of her construction there in 1831 until 1847. At some time during that sixteen-year stretch one T. L. Albro shipped aboard the vessel. Whether Albro was a master whaleman or a bungler at his job is unknown. What is certain, however, is that he deserves to be ranked among the best of American scrimshanders currently identified, an honor amply earned by the carving of a large sperm whale tooth [27] now in our collection. And whereas the Englishman Roderick used only one side of a tooth for his work, Albro left scarcely a single square inch unadorned.

What is clearly the front is deeply engraved with a whaling scene not unlike some others examined thus far. A finely etched portrait of the *John Coggeshall* appears at the butt end, five whaleboats occupy the center, and "French Rock" is placed near the tip. This is the same rockpile previously noted on the whaleship *Swift*'s walrus tusk [22].

Positioned dead center and incised in bold, shaded capital letters is the name "T. L. ALBRO." Based on current evidence this is believed to be Thomas L. Albro, a mariner born in 1806 in Portsmouth, Rhode Island. Completing this side of the tooth is an engraved "Sperm Whale" and the legend "Ship John Coggeshall of Newport, R. I."

The reverse of the tooth [28] is devoted to scenes of three whaleships, or possibly three different views of the *John Coggeshall*. A cutting-in scene is particularly interesting in that the suspended cutting stage or platform from which the large blanket pieces are cut is positioned somewhat aft of its usual location amidships. Port broadside and stern views complete this rather worn scene, presided over by Old Sol himself, peeking out from behind a cloud.

Obviously not one to waste space, Albro could not resist decorating the long bottom edge of his tooth [29] with various denizens of the deep, including "Pilot Fish, Dolphin, Blackfish, Billfish, Flying Fish, Albacore," a sea turtle, and a "Sea Serpent." Albro probably recorded the species he observed while the *John Coggeshall* cruised tropical waters. Francis A. Olmsted in his 1841 work *Incidents of a Whaling Voyage,* for example, reported seeing many of these same creatures.

A Yale graduate, Olmsted sailed aboard the New London whaleship *North America* from 1839 to 1841 in a futile effort to improve his fragile health. While in the Pacific he noted:

There are several varieties of fish that accompany ships, the most common of which, are the *albacore* and *bonetta*, or "skip jack," as he is called by the sailors. Their favorite position is a few yards in advance of the ship, and as she moves steadily forward . . . they glide along gracefully from side to side of her track, now leaping in merry gambols high out of the sea, then darting forward they cut the water after the flying fish, with their eye fixed upon their trembling victim. . . .7

That Albro's inclusion of a sea turtle in his menagerie is of more than passing significance is suggested by another entry in Olmsted's voluminous notebook: "We have taken several fine turtles within a few days, weighing from fifty to eighty pounds

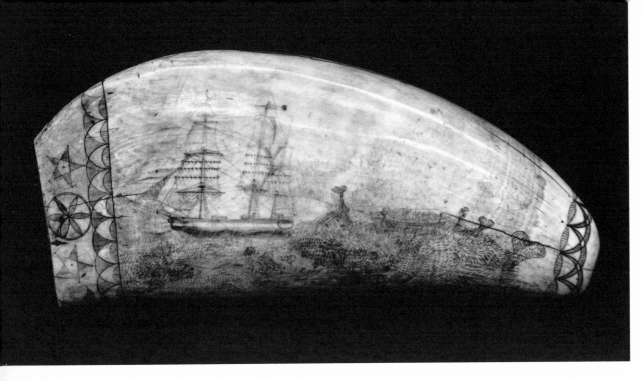

30. Captain Benjamin W. Bradford engraved this tooth aboard the whaler *Canton Packet* in the early 1830s, 8½ in. (21.6 cm.). *Source:* Museum purchase, 82.2

each, which make a very pleasant interlude in our accustomed fare."[8] Fresh seafood was always a treat for a crew living on monotonous, often spoiled, provisions.

At the same time that the *John Coggeshall* was whaling out of Newport, another Rhode Island craft, the *Canton Packet* of nearby Bristol, was also active in the whale hunt. In November 1832 the 312-ton ship, under the command of Benjamin W. Bradford, slipped down Narragansett Bay bound on a cruise to the Pacific.

During the thirty-seven-month-long voyage, Captain Bradford labored on an immense sperm whale tooth [30], which he presented to his wife's parents upon his return home in 1835, and which remained in the same family for nearly 150 years. One side depicts a broadside view of an American warship, while the opposite face is devoted to a scene Bradford knew only too well – the sperm whale hunt. A full-rigged whaleship, probably

his own *Canton Packet,* lies in the distance, while a trio of her whaleboats attacks a group of eleven whales. The sea fairly boils as whales surface and dive in a concerted effort to avoid the harpoons and killing lances. Several patches of red ink betray serious wounds. Bradford's use of short incised dashes – "stipple" engraving – in portions of the water communicates all the more the pandemonium in the foreground.

The scrimshander initialed his tooth along the bottom edge and included, like Albro, a serpent. Both tip and butt ends are encircled with overlapping scalloped borders that, along with the additional geometric imagery of stars, crescents, and rosettes at the butt end, testify to the captain's skill with drawing compass.

· 48 ·

Vessels

A considerable amount of decorative scrimshaw is devoted to marine topics other than strictly whaling activities. For example, the whaling vessel itself was a familiar subject, yet complex enough to satisfy any scrimshander's artistic ambitions. Add to this the many other types of merchant and naval vessels, especially during the nineteenth century, and the potential for ship portraiture becomes enormous.

Even newly shipped "green hands" soon became familiar enough with details of ship construction and rigging to be able to depict with reasonable fidelity their own craft as well as others encountered during a voyage. Some experienced scrimshanders, or those with natural artistic talent, were capable of producing ship portraits of high quality and accuracy.

Whaling craft in general did not receive the kind of attention paid to swift packets and clippers, whose images were reproduced on canvas, paper, and wood by trained artists. Thus in some cases our only clue to a vessel's appearance is provided by the handiwork of an anonymous shipboard artist, the scrimshander.

The engraver of one large sperm whale tooth [31] went to great pains to capture the details of the full-rigged American ship at the center of the scene. Shrouds, ratlines, and sails are quite distinguishable. The topsail schooner outward bound at the right edge is equally well done, while the lighthouse to the left serves to balance the scene. Heavily stylized water completes the composition of this busy view. The U.S. flag next to the lighthouse indicates an American setting, though it is impossible to pinpoint the exact locale. This freehand effort contrasts with a careful rendering of a large public building on the reverse, undoubtedly copied from an illustration.

The New Bedford whaling bark *Maria* was one of the oldest surviving whalers by the time of the Civil War, having been built in 1782. An interesting oblique bow view of this venerable vessel is found on a tooth [32] dated 1856. The dogged strength of bluff-bowed whalers like the *Maria* is apparent in this rendering, believed by some to have been copied from an engraving in a periodical like *Harper's Weekly*.[9] This somewhat romantic style of work, characterized by dramatic bow views of onrushing

31. Vessel portraits were a popular subject for scrimshanders. Above, a boldly engraved craft, possibly a packet ship, returning home, 7⅜ in. (18.7 cm.). Below, a more delicate rendering by a scrimshander identified only as "B A," 6⅜ in. (16.2 cm.). *Sources:* New England Savings Bank, 39.860; Miss Joanna Burnet, 41.42

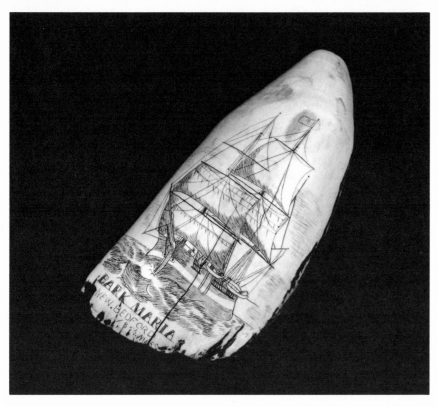

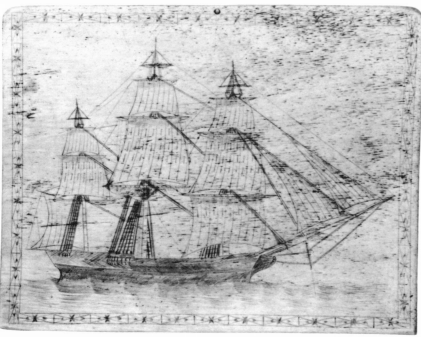

vessels with clouds of canvas set, is more commonly found on
pieces done beginning late in the nineteenth century. Its popularity continues today.

A scrimshander identified only by his initials "BA" spent a
good deal of time and effort engraving a large whale tooth [31]
with a variety of nautical and patriotic symbols. Of special note
is a very fine port broadside view of an unidentified full-rigged
ship. The sails of this vessel are painstakingly incised to illustrate
the individual canvas strips used in their construction. The
absence of whaleboats hanging off davits suggests that this ship
is either a merchantman or a warship. The use of painted false
gunports, evident here, became a fairly common practice on
merchant vessels hoping to discourage pirates, and the custom
continued long after the threat of organized piracy declined
early in the nineteenth century. Thus in the absence of other
identifying evidence we face much the same uncertainty as the
pirate in positively identifying the vessel.

Panbone slabs were particularly well suited to large-scale
vessel portraiture. The large area and flat surface characteristic
of this whalebone was utilized to good effect by many scrimshanders. Broadside views predominate, not surprisingly, since
most slabs were cut rectangular in shape. Illustrative of this type
of work is an engraved starboard view of a full-rigged merchant
ship [33], probably dating from the second quarter of the
nineteenth century. Like scrimshander "BA" this artist has care-

34. A piece of whale or porpoise panbone provides the "canvas" for this superb portrait of a small merchant vessel, 5¼ x 10½ in. (13.4 x 26.7 cm.). *Source:* Charles E. White, 39.1960

fully included sail and rigging details on the unidentified vessel. Touches of red ink highlight portions of the hull. An elaborate border of linked rectangles frames this 6½ by 8⅞ inch scene, and a single hole pierced at the top indicates that it once hung on a wall.

It is truly unfortunate that the creator of the next panbone ship portrait [34] remains unknown, save for the initials "JII"

etched on the reverse. Instead of cutting a slab of bone our scrimshander simply cut off the last 10½ inches of the jawbone of a porpoise or small whale and used the material in its natural state. The resulting slightly convex surface appears to have in no way confounded the artist's obvious talents. Engraved in full broadside prospect is a small full-rigged ship of the late eighteenth or early nineteenth century. The hull is a bit chunky,

and a prominent false stem rises from the waterline, ending in a small carved scroll billethead. The rig, while quite full, has not reached the lofty heights characteristic of square riggers by the mid-1800s. Like Burdett and Albro both, this scrimshander has opted to incise portions of his work, notably the hull, quite deeply; they are then heavily inked, resulting in an added sense of depth.

As in the case of Ephraim Dodge's baleen engraving, vessel portraits are sometimes found in the midst of other subject matter. Such is the case with a superb tooth [35] featuring the 335-ton Newport, Rhode Island, whaleship *Mechanic*. Like the *John Coggeshall*, the *Mechanic* was built in Newport. She sailed from that port throughout her entire career, 1834-1861, finally being scuttled in 1862 as part of the Union Navy's "Stone Fleet" effort to blockade the harbor at Charleston, South Carolina.

The broadside portrait of the *Mechanic* is placed within an elaborate circular sawtooth border, in turn surrounded by patriotic symbols and allegorical figures of Plenty and Justice. Beneath the vessel's name is the notation "H. Daggett Comm[ndr.]," undoubtedly a reference to Henry Daggett, listed in customs house records as the ship's first master, 1834-1838.[10] The reverse side features an American ship of the line likewise framed within an elaborate circle. Patriotic and sentimental devices complete the scene.

It is quite possible that this unknown scrimshander produced more work, possibly on the same voyage. A busk in the Kendall Whaling Museum and another *Mechanic* tooth in a private collection share several common elements with the Museum's example, viz: a banner reading "FORGET ME NOT"; an identi-

35. The whaleship *Mechanic* is surrounded by geometric, patriotic, and allegorical imagery on this sperm whale tooth, 7⅝ in. (19.3 cm.). *Source:* Harold H. Kynett, 55.1037

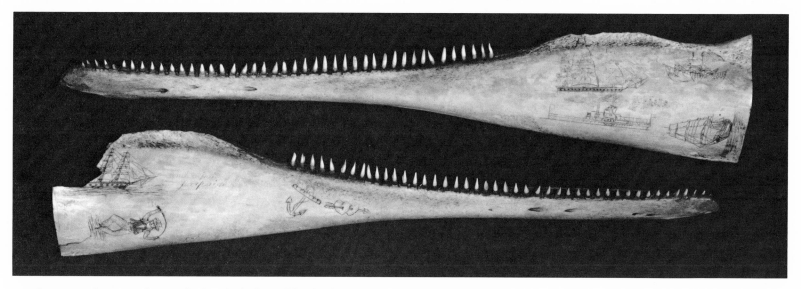

36. An unusual engraved porpoise jaw includes a sidewheel steamer in addition to portraits of square riggers, 2¾ x 14⁵/₁₆ in. (7.0 x 36.4 cm.). *Source:* John Alsop, 75.6ab

cal eagle with shield bearing an anchor, symbolic of Rhode Island's state motto "Hope"; and another banner with the national motto curiously worded "PLURIBUS E UNUM." The privately owned *Mechanic* tooth has the name "Wardwell" faintly written on it in ink; but insufficient data exists to determine whether this refers to the scrimshander.

Porpoise jaws, with a surface similar to that of whale panbone, were only occasionally used as a medium for scrimshaw. The Seaport's one complete example [36], however, has been fairly well covered with a variety of nautical and patriotic motifs. Most numerous of these are an assortment of engraved merchant vessels, including an early sidewheel steamer named the *Globe*. The jaw is in two pieces, each about fourteen inches long, and the engravings are colored in sepia ink. With its many needle-sharp teeth intact, the jaw possesses a sinister appear-

ance. And though himself unidentified, the scrimshander thought it wise to note that the item was the "under jaw of a porpose."

Not surprisingly British scrimshanders also found occasion to portray vessels on whale teeth and bone. One striking example of British work is a 7 by 9¾ inch oval panbone plaque [37] engraved with an unidentified British whaleship plowing along under full sail, a whaleboat clearly visible hanging on her port quarter. The myriad particulars of sail and rigging are accurately presented; indeed, tiny drilled depressions mark deadeyes and sail reef points, which details are then enhanced after inking. Such technical competence and pride of workmanship suggest an artist who was also a knowledgeable mariner. Now this same experienced seaman has employed a bit of patriotic artistic license in putting Britain's merchant marine ensign in full view,

· 53 ·

37. The scrimshander's thorough knowledge of rigging is apparent in this unusual oval panbone view of a British whaleship, 7 x 9¾ in. (17.8 x 24.8 cm.). *Source:* Charles E. White, 39.1961

an impossible feat on a square rigger sailing, as in this case, on a port tack with the wind nearly astern. Well, perhaps there were "locally variable" winds that day.

The ships *Medina* and *Warren Hastings* share equal billing on a large sperm whale tooth whose creator is identified only by the initials "TA." Though it is unknown just who "TA" was, it is fairly certain that he was English, as the *Warren Hastings* was the name of at least three successive British East Indiamen, large armed merchantmen that plied the trade route between Britain and her Indian empire. The three vessels of this name were built between 1782 and 1809. The engraved *Medina* on the tooth is quite possibly the 469-ton English ship of that name built in 1811. Further suggesting an East Indian connection are the engraved letters "HEIC," thought to mean "Honourable East

India Company," the English firm granted what amounted to a monopoly on the lucrative trade with Britain's East Indian possessions. Completing the tooth is an engraved Admiralty-style anchor and elaborate geometrical border around the tip.

Home and Family

Whatever a man's reason for shipping aboard a whaler, whether simply desire for profit and adventure, an opportunity for travel, or even the hope of improving health and stamina, it is likely that thoughts of home were never far from mind. It is probably even safe to say that many who signed on for a voyage

38. A plaintive verse accompanies its author's self-portrait on a tooth engraved during an 1847 whaling voyage, 5½ in. (14.0 cm.). *Source:* Mrs. Raynham Townshend, 47.1364

39. Whaleman Charles Hewit etched his Lyme, Connecticut, home on a small busk in 1840, 6¹/₁₆ in. (15.4 cm.).
Source: Charles E. White, 39.1915

in order to escape something at home, the law perhaps, or domestic perturbations, sooner or later felt a longing for people and places left behind. The long periods of idleness encountered on voyages of three or four years' duration allowed plenty of opportunity for lonely reflection, much of it centering on home.

The time-killing quality of scrimshaw, as noted, was appreciated by many whalemen. That it occasionally became an outlet for expressing homesickness and the pain of separation from family and friends is equally true and understandable. The classic form of this sentiment is expressed on a sperm whale tooth [38] engraved in 1847 "Off Samoa." Etched alongside the self-portrait of a young sailor is the plea:

> When I'm away on the restless sea
> I hope my love, youll think of me.

This piece illustrates the point, mentioned in Chapter 1, that scrimshaw items were occasionally intended as gifts for people back home. Thus both the sentiment of and motivation for this particular tooth are linked to the thought of home.

Although busks, those often decorated bone or baleen stays intended for women's corsets, will be considered in the chapter on utilitarian scrimshaw, several small examples, probably intended primarily as keepsakes, deserve mention here. One whalebone busk, probably made by the shipbound "J. M." for his "F. L." ashore, states simply: "WHILE/AT SEA/THINK OF/

ME." Since the verse is signed "JO," an informal abbreviation of "John," it is most probable that John M. meant to say: "While *I'm* at sea think of me."

Yet another undersize whalebone busk [39] is engraved on both sides with a variety of scenes and information. The front is illustrated with both a brig at "SEA" and a two-story frame "HOME" with a prominent tree alongside. A wharf scene in the center provides a logical transition between the two elements. From the reverse we learn that our scrimshander is "Charles Hewit" of Lyme, Connecticut, who made the busk in 1840 from the bone of a sperm whale that yielded his ship one hundred barrels of oil. Even in the midst of successful hunting, though, Hewit was clearly thinking of home.

Occasionally a matched pair of teeth appear that share certain decorative elements. Such an ivory duo [40] in the collection illustrates what might be termed a "his and her" arrangement. A sailor, "J M," invested quite a bit of time carving and engraving a sperm whale tooth. A full-rigged ship and waterfront scene

40. This matched pair of teeth was possibly once part of a watch stand, 6³/₄ in. (17.2 cm.). *Source:* Charles E. White, 39.1754, 39.1755

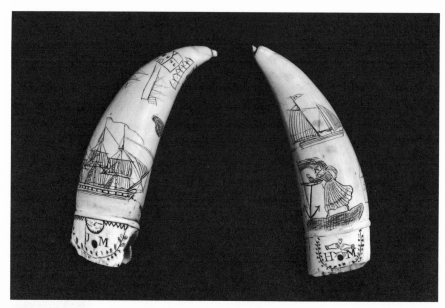

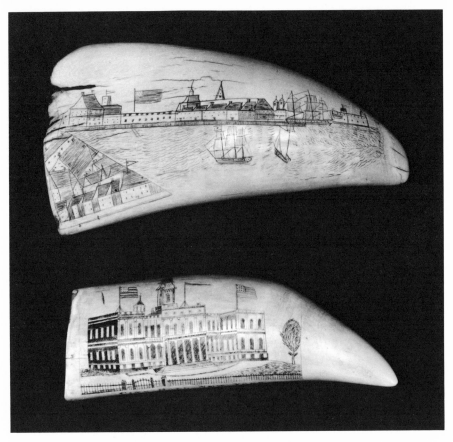

41. Above is a view believed to be Boston Harbor, 8¼ in. (21.0 cm.).
Below, "CITY HALL NEW YORK" has been faithfully copied from an illustration
onto a sperm whale tooth, 7⅜ in. (18.7 cm.). *Sources:* Harold H. Kynett, 55.1038;
New England Savings Bank, 39.860

appeared on the front, with a lighthouse and keeper's cottage
perched on a rocky headland decorating the reverse. "JM" went
a bit further by carving the tip of the tooth into a tiny knob, and
carving a raised lip or ring around the tooth near the base. As a
final touch, at the base of the tooth he added his initials,
surrounded by a branch and leaf design, to which was added a
small vignette showing two hands reaching out, almost touch-
ing.

No doubt "JM" had plenty of time on his hands, as well as
another, nearly identical, tooth with which to work. And no
doubt, too, the brilliant idea occurred to him to carve a mate for
his mate; that is to say, a companion tooth for his wife, "HM,"
who anxiously awaited his return from the sea. Thus we find
"HM" standing on the shore beside an anchor and U.S. flag,
gazing straight out to sea. When the teeth are arranged side by
side with the carved tips pointing toward each other, "HM" is
able to peer across the gap directly at her spouse's ship, a
convenient arrangement indeed. A schooner and an unfinished
house complete the scene. The tooth is carved in an identical
manner as the first, and the initials "HM" now reside within the
branch and leaf border. The outstretched hands are there too,
this time accompanied by a heart, a clear indication of her
husband's feelings while separated by great distance.

An examination of these curved teeth, with their pierced
bases and curious carved knobs at the tips, suggests that they
were designed to stand upright, attached to some type of base.
The arch formed by the inward curving of the teeth might have
been completed by some center piece, perhaps of wood. Such
an arrangement could be used as a decorative clock or watch
stand, though this is speculative.

Engraving of famous or just locally familiar landmarks was
another expression of home that turns up on decorative scrimshaw. Sometimes, as in the case of one tooth [41], a published
illustration served as the guide. Here is "CITY HALL NEW

42 (left). A superbly engraved "Family Tooth" provides an unusual
genealogical record of the Daniel McKenzie family of New Bedford,
7¼ in. (18.4 cm.). *Source:* Mrs. Alexander O. Vietor, 81.64.19

43 (right). Reverse of the McKenzie "Family Tooth," possibly
the work of Daniel McKenzie, Jr., 7¼ in. (18.4 cm.). *Source:*
Mrs. Alexander O. Vietor, 81.64.19

YORK," a stately neoclassical edifice bounded by an iron spike fence. Even if the scrimshander were not from New York, this slice of home might appeal to him as more familiar and comfortable than the native architecture of the South Seas, or wherever he might have found himself.

More than a few Boston men tried their hand at whaling, and it is possible that one of them painstakingly engraved the bird's-eye view of the harbor found on a very wide sperm whale tooth [41]. Though identified as Boston harbor in the donor's records, the location is not specified on the tooth itself, leaving the researcher to fend for himself. The presence of what looks to be a fortification, flying an oversize U.S. flag, in the midst of other large structures suggests a military setting, perhaps the Boston Navy Yard in Charlestown. There appears to be a large frigate at the right, which would make sense if this were a naval installation. The adjacent waterfront area with its closely packed buildings offers no other clues to the scene's locale.

Home and family receive undisputed top billing on what is almost certainly a unique piece of scrimshaw [42, 43]. Engraved on a handsome sperm whale tooth is the genealogical record of the Daniel and Phebe McKenzie family for the period 1794-1834. Elaborate floral and squiggle designs surround the entries on what the scrimshander has termed the "Family Tooth." Using a total of at least eight different printed and cursive lettering styles the chronicler notes the following:

> Danl Mc.Kenzie born May 1st AD. 1794
> Phebe McKenzie born May 5th AD. 1796
> Were Married February 10th 1818
> NANCY MC.KENZIE. born October 24 AD. 1818.
> Daniel Mc.Kenzie Jr, born July 10 A.D. 1821.
> Mary & Adeline twins born July 2 A.D. 1824
> Adeline died June 2 AND Mary died August 29 1825.
> Alexander McKenzie born A.D. 1830
> MARY MC.KENZIE born A.D. 1834

Research indicates that this record refers to the Daniel McKenzie family of New Bedford, Massachusetts. Captain Daniel McKenzie commanded such whaleships as the *Minerva Smyth, Pacific, Samuel Robertson,* and *Caroline* during the years 1820-1846. His son, Daniel, Jr. (1821-1862), accompanied him on an around-the-world whaling voyage aboard the *Samuel Robertson* during the years 1837-1840. While on board, the teenage McKenzie kept a journal, now in the collection of the New Bedford Whaling Museum, featuring beautiful, practiced handwriting and superb watercolor illustrations of landfalls and other observations. There is the tantalizing possibility that young McKenzie engraved the "Family Tooth," probably with the aid of a copybook, and perhaps on this very whaling voyage. The tooth's uncertain authorship notwithstanding, this piece remains a singular example of the scrimshander's art.

Adding to the pain of leave-taking, occasionally illustrated by the scrimshander with a tearful "Sailor's Farewell" scene, was the general uncertainty of life in the nineteenth century. The dangers of whaling and the sea were apparent and the risks recognized and accepted. But death could and often did lay claim to one or more loved ones while a whaleman was at sea; and it is probable that he viewed his impending return home with a mixture of excitement and foreboding.

Infant mortality was an all too familiar fact of life, as the McKenzie "Family Tooth" suggests. Captain McKenzie was in the Pacific commanding the *Minerva Smyth* when his twin daughters died in the summer of 1825. Compounding the tragedy is the distressing possibility that he had sailed on the same voyage just before the July 1824 birth of the girls, which would mean that he had never even seen Mary and Adeline.

The sobering realization of the tenuousness of life, combined with the widespread Victorian preoccupation with death and loneliness, accounts for a certain poignancy in the depiction of home and family by some scrimshanders. Weeping willows, memorial monuments, and tombs surrounded with mourners occasionally appear on teeth and like items. Curiously, though, the Museum's collection presently lacks any strictly decorative pieces with such somber domestic overtones.

Women

Human nature being what it is, many shipbound lads let their minds wander toward thoughts of what was then widely described as the "fairer sex." And why not, since so many of the crewmen were in their teens and twenties,[11] fully aware of the special deprivations attendant upon long whaling voyages. W. S. Maxfield, in 1852 a young crewman aboard the New Bedford whaleship *Niger,* confided to his journal his thoughts on the matter.

Strong breezes from the north. Scrubbed decks in the morning. O, how I wish I was at home today to go to meeting, and tonight also for to see the girls. That's what I like, is the girls—girls forever for me, I say... So ends the day—but homesick.[12]

What was especially depressing for young Maxfield was the fact that he had been on board ship only four days. How fortunate that he did not then know that 3½ years would elapse before he would again "see the girls" of home.

With women, or the glaring lack thereof, on their minds it comes as no great shock to learn that whalemen often depicted them on decorative scrimshaw. Walter K. Earle in his 1957 work *Scrimshaw: Folk Art of the Whalers* asserts that the human figure was probably the single most popular decorative motif.[13] And portraits of women, usually anonymous, constitute a large portion of such work.

The sources for many of these pieces appear to have been printed illustrations, since most which have been studied exhibit telltale pin-prick outlines. But why so many women's portraits copied so carefully? Whaleman-artist Clifford W. Ashley felt quite strongly that in this area alone did the otherwise versatile scrimshander feel inadequate to the task, and thus borrowed freely from available illustrations.[14]

A variety of illustrated periodicals containing potential graphics were available by the mid-1850s. *Harper's Weekly, Harper's New Monthly Magazine, Ballou's Pictorial Drawing Room Companion,* and others were filled with engraved illustrations, including many depicting the latest fashions from the Continent. Such feminine finery, modeled as it was by the fairest women the magazine artist could create, provided much grist for the scrimshander's mill. Whether carried aboard by a crewman or provided as "proper" reading material by the captain's wife or some seamen's charitable organization,[15] it appears obvious that such publications found a ready audience among scrimshanders, literate and otherwise.

The periodical perhaps most closely associated with scrimshaw portraits of "fashionable" women was *Godey's Lady's Book,* founded in 1830. Complementing the usual fashion engravings were hand-colored "fashion plates" of remarkable quality, just the thing for an ambitious scrimshander interested in expanding his repertoire. Indeed, fashionable women appearing on scrimshaw are often automatically referred to as "Godey's Ladies." To date, however, not one piece in the Museum's collection can be positively traced to a specific *Godey* illustration. A recent study has found this to be the case in many other collections as well.[16]

Sperm whale teeth were the favorite medium for women's portraits, nearly always engraved so as to be viewed standing upright. In this vertical format even full-length portraits could be accommodated. A fine half-length engraving of a young woman graces one tooth [44] in the collection. Identified by the scrimshander simply as "JANE," this woman wears a very stylish bonnet, quite a popular article judging from its frequent appearance in other women's portraits. So carefully did the artist follow his paper model that only under the closest scrutiny are the tiny pin pricks detectable.

An exceedingly fine job of engraving characterizes a tooth [44] with a full-length portrait of a stylishly attired young woman. This clear side view allows much of the woman's voluminous garment to be seen, accented by her tiny waist, an effect no doubt aided by baleen corset stays. Headgear, evident in many similar portraits of the period, here takes the form of a stylish ribboned hat rather than a bonnet. A crosshatched floor lends a sense of depth to the scene.

Touches of color appear on a number of our etched ivory women. One tooth [44], whose portrait at first glance looks for all the world like a European monarch in her royal finery, is

44. A Victorian fashion show, featuring, left to right, a fan and ribboned hat, 6¼ in. (15.9 cm.); a touch of royal elegance, 5⁷⁄₁₆ in. (13.8 cm.); the popular bonnet, 3⁷⁄₈ in. (9.8 cm.); and the soft pastel look, 5⁷⁄₈ in. (14.9 cm.). *Sources:* Charles E. White, 39.1757; Mrs. Lawrence M. C. Smith, 57.710; Mrs. Raynham Townshend, 47.1375, 47.1351

highlighted by blue-green coloring on the woman's collar and a red flower visible in her hair. A quick perusal of mid-nineteenth-century magazines will show that such elaborate dress was all the rage among those elements of society who could afford it. As with most works of this type, there is no clue as to the engraver's identity.

Women were often pictured as being lonely, pensive, and generally sad in period illustrations, a reflection perhaps of Victorian literary and social tastes.[17] It is only natural then that such an image is found mirrored in the work of the scrimshander. One tooth [44] is particularly illustrative of this treatment. Here a lone woman is seen standing and holding the ever popular bonnet cap, her head bowed down. Her face reflects an air of resignation to some unspecified fate. Complementing this lovely woman, with her almost classical facial profile, is a full dress so subtly inked that the red, green, and blue colors have a pastel quality to them. Unfortunately, neither the artist nor the source of the original illustration is known.

One of the Seaport's few scrimshaw teeth with a multiple portrait [45] shows an unusual scene of two women walking away, their backs to the viewer. One is quite tall, the other short of stature; and besides short dresses and bonnets, both women are quite obviously wearing bloomers, the loose trousers worn under a short skirt that hit the fashion world in the nineteenth century. Named after Amelia J. Bloomer (1818-1894), a social reformer and early suffragette, bloomers were widely ridiculed by men, as were many of the women activists who first wore them in the 1840s. Perhaps our unknown scrimshander was making his own statement on the subject when he first sat down with this tooth.

A superbly engraved portrait fills one side of a large sperm whale tooth [45] belonging to the Museum. The three-

45. More women's styles including, from left, a fashionable cloak, 6⅝ in. (16.9 cm.); bloomers, 4¾ in. (12.1 cm.); a flowing dress, 5½ in. (14.0 cm.); and a study in geometric patterns, 6 in. (15.2 cm.). *Sources:* Charles E. White, 39.1753, 39.1722; Mrs. Raynham Townshend, 47.1358; Charles E. White, 39.1769

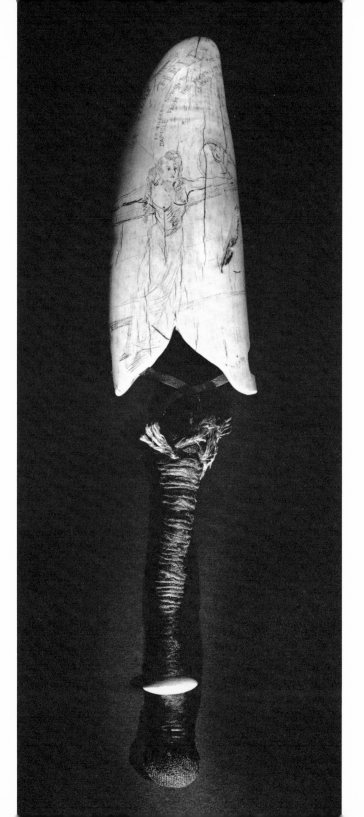

quarter-length view shows a beautifully dressed woman with long flowing hair, striking a rather thoughtful pose as she sits in a garden. As usual she is alone and apparently preoccupied with one matter or another. Red ink is selectively used to highlight the flowers behind her as well as the bow attached to the bodice of her dress.

That scarves were popular at some time during the last century is evident from the fashionable woman incised on yet another whale tooth [45]. The solid-color scarf contrasts vividly with the dress, whose puffy sleeves and full flare allowed this scrimshander to achieve an elaborate pattern of contrasting lines and dots. As in the previous work this woman, though alone, is in the company of nature in the form of a treelike flowering plant. The lower quality evident in the engraving of a man on the reverse of this tooth suggests that the woman was the primary subject for this artist.

Of all the fashionable women depicted on scrimshaw in the collection, one engraved portrait above all suggests the image of a "Godey's Lady" [45]. The minute detail captured in the dress as well as the professional bearing assumed by the woman indicate that a high-quality illustration served as the model, to be attached to the tooth and outlined with pin pricks. A rich blue colors the major portion of the dress, while a handkerchief and the ubiquitous bonnet cap complete the work. Whether this is indeed a *Godey* portrait or not remains to be learned, but the key elements of this type of work—style, detail, proportion, and color—are all found in this piece.

Given the kind of emotional pressures inherent in long periods of shipboard isolation, it would not be a bit surprising to find some improper depictions of women on scrimshaw. Yet

46. Washington Foster's unusual whale tooth club, 13 in. (33.0 cm.). *Source:* Charles E. White, 39.2077

pornographic or vulgar pieces are very rare. One study recently proposed several possible explanations for this somewhat surprising state of affairs. First, the fact that some pieces were created as gifts for family or close friends made erotic items less likely. Victorian morality frowned on sexually explicit material. Second, many God-fearing captains would no doubt disapprove of such work being done on board their ships, leading to possible confiscation and disposal of offensive work. Third, a scrimshander might well have tossed such pieces overboard before arriving back home.[18]

Only one piece in the Museum's collection comes close to being erotic in nature and, curiously enough, the scrimshander sailed from Mystic. A Mystic-built schooner, variously spelled *Emeline* and *Emmeline,* sailed in July 1843 on a sea elephanting voyage to the Indian Ocean. Upon reaching what were probably the Crozet Islands, the crew went to work slaying the huge animals, known also as elephant seals, and trying out their thick blubber for oil. It was while on board ship that one Washington Foster began to fashion a whale tooth club [46] using a flexible, rope-bound handle. The good condition of the object suggests that it was never used as a club. But it is safe to say that it was most certainly an interesting conversation piece.

The front of the tooth carries Foster's name in bold capital letters, along with the scattered notations "SHIP [*sic*]/EMMELINE," "Mistic Conn./1843," "CROISITTES," and "FOR SEA ELEPHANT/OIL." This is perfectly acceptable material for any scrimshander.

Engraved on the reverse, however, is a semi-clad young woman, bound to a ship's rail, piteously wailing:

> HELP HELP HELP
> IS THERE NOWON TO SAVE THE FAIR
> DAMSLE FROM THE FREEBOOTERS
> LEWD EMBRASE.

Foster obviously possessed a fairly active imagination, and undoubtedly this item generated a considerable amount of interest whenever it was shown. But our scrimshander was a man of wider talents as well. He kept a lavishly illustrated journal, now in the collection of the New Bedford Whaling Museum, which chronicles the year-long voyage of the *Emeline.* As talented an individual as he evidently was, however, he will probably be best remembered for this unusual scrimshaw effort.

Characters, Famous and Otherwise

The fashionable woman was by no means the sole subject of scrimshanders' portraits. Historical and literary characters were also transferred to bone and tooth. Here again, though, the sperm whale tooth was far and away the most popular vehicle for scrimshaw artists. But whereas most of our fashionable women were copied from illustrations using the pin-prick method, a number of these other works were freehanded.

Of all the characters known to seamen perhaps the most familiar was the seaman himself. Yet of the many scrimshaw portraits in the collection only a handful depict the mariner. Already noted is the lack of closeup deck views showing shipboard work, for example. In most of the scenes where individuals can be observed they are merely "stick people" visible on shipboard or so much human confetti strewn about the remains of a stove whaleboat. A few scrimshanders, however, took the time to depict themselves, either as they were or as people imagined them to be.

We have already seen the self-portrait of one young sailor who wrote some verse "Off Samoa" in 1847 [38]. A somewhat more romantic view etched on a sperm whale tooth [47] shows a youthful "JACK TAR" on a wharf carefully coiling line in his

47. Scrimshaw seamen: a stylish "JACK TAR" handles lines, 4 3/8 in.
(11.1 cm.); and a Navy rating proudly waves the flag, 6 in. (15.2 cm.).
Sources: Mrs. Raynham Townshend, 47.1373; Charles E. White, 39.1756

hands. His clothing, which includes shirt and tie, vest, tarred
hat, and bell bottom trousers, was probably suggested by a
book illustration of some type.

Though patriotic motifs will be examined later, one tooth
[47] with strong national overtones deserves mention here. A
very fine side view of an American seaman, perhaps a Navy
rating, commands the viewer's attention. There is nothing more
patriotic than a thirteen-star American flag, and our sailor's
pose seems to bear this out as he proudly holds the staff of just
such a banner. The maritime connection is completed by the
iron folding-stock anchor at the seaman's feet. The strong
patriotic flavor of this piece and the appearance of an improved
style of anchor suggests that the tooth dates to the Civil War,

when a sense of national identity and pride ran deep in the
North.

A more free-spirited rendering of the American seaman appears on one side of the porpoise jaw [48] mentioned previously. The sailor seems to be dancing a jig or hornpipe with
wild abandon, all the while brandishing a sword or whip over
his head. Unfortunately, no explanation of this rather excited
behavior is offered by our anonymous artist.

Children were depicted as near-precious objects by sentimental Victorians, so what could be more appealing than a vision of
a young sailor lad struggling for survival against all odds. Such
is the image beautifully engraved on a spectacular nine-inch-
long sperm whale tooth [49]. "The Sailor Boy," as he is identified, is seen clambering up the ratlines on a stormy night, the
scene aptly described by the verse

48. An American sailor
dancing a jig. Detail from
an engraved porpoise jaw.
See Figure 36. *Source:* John
Alsop, 75.6ab

Though the strained mast quivers as a reed
And the rent canvas fluttering strew the gale,
Still must I on . . . BYRON

This elaborate vignette is framed by the transom of a large sailing ship.

Though the scrimshander's skill is of the highest order, the artist did not concoct this scene on his own. Instead he carefully copied the engraved frontispiece [50] from a book succinctly titled *Shipwrecks and Disasters at Sea, or Historical Narratives of the Most Noted Calamities, and Providential Deliverances from Fire and Famine on the Ocean, with a Sketch of the Various Expedients for Preserving the Lives of Mariners By the Aid of Life Boats, Life Preservers, &c.* First appearing in 1836, this compact book, compiled by Charles Ellms, continued to be published until at least 1860. Of added interest is the fact that the Museum also has

50. Book frontispiece supplied the model for "The Sailor Boy" tooth. From *Shipwrecks and Disasters at Sea*, 1836.

49. An unusually fine example of scrimshaw: "The Sailor Boy," 9 in. (22.8 cm.). *Source:* Museum purchase, 74.691

51 (left). A pin-pricked "Alwilda," the female pirate,
striking her customary pose. Detail from a walrus tusk.
Source: Mrs. Raynham Townshend, 47.1345

52 (right). Woman buccaneer "Fanny Campbell" was inspired
by the literary success of "Alwilda," 5⅛ in. (13.0 cm.).
Source: Charles E. White, 39.1804

an unsigned nineteenth-century oil portrait of this "Sailor Boy,"
which almost certainly predates the book engraving.

A fictional character quite popular with scrimshanders was
Alwilda, the female pirate. Contributing to the popularity of
Alwilda was the combination of excitement, romance, and that
sure-fire literary device—mistaken identity—used in the plot. As

a skilled mariner, Alwilda was adopted by the sailor as one of his
own breed, an appeal evident in the many scrimshaw portraits
of this woman sea rover. Her story and illustration were found
in a work entitled *The Pirates Own Book,* published at least as
early as 1837. Among the stories contained therein was that of
the princess Alwilda who, in order to avoid an arranged marriage, runs off to sea dressed as a man. In time she becomes a
feared pirate captain and is finally captured in battle by her
erstwhile intended, Prince Alf. A change of heart leads Alwilda
to wed Alf on the spot, with everyone living happily ever after.

Alwilda is similarly represented on two walrus tusks in the
collection. As depicted [51] she is dressed in man's pants and
wears a flaring, skirtlike jacket. Over her capped head she holds
a saber, and in her belt are tucked a dagger and pistol. Well
armed indeed is the lady. Both pieces include a variety of other,
unrelated designs. The tusk not illustrated is noted as having
been done on board the New Bedford whaler *Isabella* in 1855 by
a scrimshander identified only as "E. T." or "E. P."

So popular was the concept of the female pirate that before
long an Alwilda clone appeared in the guise of "Fanny
Campbell, The Female Pirate Captain." A pamphlet by the same
name, written by Murray Ballou Maturius (1820-1895) under
the pen name "Lieutenant Murray," apparently used a suspi-
ciously similar plot and illustration. The one piece in the collection, a tooth, on which Fanny appears [52], shows that her
costume was certainly inspired by Alwilda's. Only minor differences like the position of the saber, the addition of the pirate
flag, and the greater amount of firepower tucked in her belt
serve to distinguish the two female buccaneers.[19] Based on a
check of the original Fanny Campbell illustration it appears that
this scrimshander desired a bit more realistic background and so
added a large capstan to the scene. In addition touches of red
ink highlight Fanny's long jacket.

Among a scrimshander's other sources of famous characters is Scripture. A partially clad Eve, for example, graces one side of a whale tooth. As she ponders her fateful choice the serpent is seen coiled about a tree, most likely *the* tree.

Literature provides other figures, including Prince Hamlet clothed in an elaborate costume of many colors. Careful cross-hatching supplies all the stage that this toothbound character will ever need.

Our own native literature is also represented on scrimshaw. A young woman, hands clasped as if in prayer or supplication, appears on a sperm whale tooth. Named "ELIZA," the portrait is possibly that of the main character in Harriet Beecher Stowe's *Uncle Tom's Cabin,* published in 1852.

A European aristocrat in full military regalia occupies one side of a whale tooth [53]. His identification as "ALEXANDER" is puzzling until on examining the reverse we find what is almost certainly a scene depicting the apotheosis of Abraham Lincoln. With the identification of Lincoln settled, "ALEXANDER" must almost certainly be the Russian Czar Alexander II (1818-1881). Alexander was hailed by many in the North for his emancipation of the serfs in 1861, though their subsequent lot did not warrant such enthusiasm. Thus we have the Russian emancipator on one side and the "Great Emancipator" on the other. And Alexander increased his popularity in the North by dispatching several naval squadrons to American ports in 1863. Though this was simply a move to protect his fleet from the threat of Anglo-French intervention in a dispute over Poland, many in the North interpreted the Russian naval visits as a show of support for the Union at a time when some feared British intervention of the side of the Confederacy.[20]

A wave of pro-Russian sentiment swept the Union side, and a good many articles were devoted to the Russian sailors and their emperor, Alexander. Most likely the scrimshander used a

53. European royalty provided subject matter for scrimshanders. At left, Napoleon riding into battle, 6 in. (15.2 cm.); and Czar Alexander II, the "Russian emancipator," 6¼ in. (15.9 cm.). *Source:* Charles E. White, 39.1797, 39.1740

newspaper or magazine illustration as a model for this royal portrait.

Another imperial figure who captured a scrimshander's imagination was Napoleon I, illustrated on a sharply curved sperm whale tooth [53]. In spite of our democratic precepts, or perhaps because of them, we Americans have always had a fascination with European royalty. Add to this Napoleon's flair for decisive military action and his enmity toward England and you have a perfect subject for an American scrimshander.

Napoleon as the man of action is the theme stressed in this particular piece of engraving. Riding uphill on a charger in the heat of battle, he is seen moving toward the French tricolor visible in the distance. Franco-American friendship is suggested by the American warship engraved on the reverse and a freehand portrait of George Washington that appears on a companion tooth to be discussed in more detail later.

Exotic Scenes & Caricatures

No matter how strong a whaleman's preoccupation with home, he could not ignore the unusual peoples, places, and sights encountered while cruising distant seas. Such novel and exotic locales provided fresh, topical material for the scrimshander.

54. Exotic sights recorded on ivory: an African witch doctor at left, 6 in. (15.2 cm.); and a tattooed Maori from New Zealand, 5⅞ in. (14.9 cm.). *Sources:* Mrs. Raynham Townshend, 47.1352; Charles E. White, 39.1772

South Sea islands and their inhabitants were prime candidates for inclusion on whalebone and ivory. One sperm whale tooth, for example, provides a fine view of an island plantation house replete with thatched roof, palm trees, and other tropical vegetation. The local flora in the scene have been inked green for added interest.

A wide variety of native peoples were encountered during globe-circling whaling voyages or long merchant cruises, and an unknown scrimshander used a whale tooth [54] to illustrate one such individual. Both facial and torsal tattooing on the native man and the British flag flying from the fort in the background suggest a New Zealand setting. The islands, first settled by the English in 1840, were inhabited by the aboriginal Maoris, who practiced such ceremonial skin illustration.

Early ventures into the Pacific in the late eighteenth century led in time to whalers and sealers penetrating the Northwest Coast areas, present-day Oregon, Washington State, British Columbia, and southern Alaska. A number of Indian tribes inhabited the area, including the seafaring Haidas, who whaled and fished from their homes on the Queen Charlotte Islands off British Columbia.

The presence of valuable fur seals and whales attracted increasing numbers of whalers, sealers, and traders during the early nineteenth century. In the 1830s the 300-ton New Bedford whaleship *Triton* apparently visited the Queen Charlotte Islands while on a Pacific cruise. A crewman, John Marshall, came across a sperm whale tooth engraved with two demons, a shark, a frog, and whales, apparently from a whale taken by the Haidas. The details of this find are sketchy, as is the explanation that Marshall engraved on the tooth. Through an early record accompanying the item we can piece together the now partially illegible entry:

Charm taken from the body of the witch doctor
of the Haidor tribe Queen Sharlot Islands
August 6. 183[?] by John Marshall
whaleship Triton.

Whether this trophy was acquired as a result of one of the armed clashes that periodically occurred between natives and whites is not known. Completing the piece is a curious metal bail handle attached in two holes drilled at the butt end of the tooth.

Some years earlier and halfway around the world another whaleman had had a close encounter with a foreign people, most probably on the west coast of Africa. Martin Snow used a sperm whale tooth [54] to record some of his experiences or observations after having been "Wrecked/−1827−/ Mombasssa/Guinea." The reverse of the tooth portrays a scarecrow-like figure dancing, with the equatorial sun peering down from above. The front of the tooth is incised with a sinister robed figure wearing an elaborate headdress and mask and standing with limbs outstretched. Two birds and what might be a frog are also visible. By way of partial explanation the castaway noted: "Dont trust this DEVIL Doctor/Martin Snow master/whaleman." This is most likely Snow's impression of a local witch doctor whom he had had the fortune, or perhaps misfortune, to meet.

The Atlantic whaling grounds off the African coast were productive for most of the nineteenth century and continued to be of some importance to the U.S. whale fishery into our own century. Whaling vessels would occasionally stop for fresh water and provisions, though Snow's visit was clearly involuntary. Curiously, Snow's memento, like John Marshall's piece, has the remains of some type of metal handle arrangement attached to it. Perhaps it was intended as a club, like Washington Foster's unusual handiwork.

Mythological creatures like "sea serpents" do not often ap-

55. A carefully pin-pricked Victorian mermaid. Detail of a large walrus tusk. *Source:* Dr. Roger N. Ryley, 59.606

pear on scrimshaw, although Albro's *John Coggeshall* tooth [29] does include a water snake so labeled. Another creature of lore, and one considerably less frightening, is the mermaid. Though clearly connected with the sea the mermaid, according to a 1976 study, appears in nautical folk art only rarely and on scrimshaw almost never.[21] The Museum, however, is fortunate enough to have a twenty-six-inch-long walrus tusk [55] engraved with a lovely Victorian mermaid. This tusk, one of a pair, was given to a Captain James Ryley by his crew about 1876. Such a presentation casts some doubt on the theory that sighting a mermaid, like killing an albatross, was regarded as a sign of impending doom.

56. A matched pair of teeth featuring caricatures. At left, a Chinese man reading, 6 in. (15.2 cm.); at right, a parody of the bloomer fashion, 6¼ in. (15.9 cm.). *Source:* Mrs. Lawrence M. C. Smith, 57.708, 57.707

Outright caricatures are fairly rare as scrimshaw motifs, but a matched pair of whale teeth in the collection illustrate well some interesting social attitudes from the last century. One piece [56] shows a seated Chinese man, wearing frock coat and cap, reading a newspaper with a magnifying lens. In what might be construed as a racist comment on the supposed true character of the "civilized" Chinese, the man's foot is pictured as that of an animal, and a tail sticks out from under the coat, suggesting a monkey or some other unflattering comparison.

The mate to this piece [56] is engraved with a rather outlandish portrait of a hen wearing a short skirt and bloomers. Sound familiar? It would appear that the scrimshander has copied an editorial cartoon, perhaps from the English magazine *Punch,* this time lampooning the bloomer fashion popular in America, and at the same time the women activists who espoused it. It would seem that this artist and the creator of the other "bloomer" tooth shared attitudes held by most men of the day.

Naval Glory

America's two wars of independence, the Revolution and the War of 1812, as well as various skirmishes with the French and the Barbary pirates in the intervening years, offered irrefutable proof of the value of naval and maritime power. In a world largely hostile to the American democratic experiment the need for naval defense was clear, if not always heeded.

The strategies of blockade and seaborne raid bedeviled the Americans in both conflicts with England. And as a leading neutral shipper, the U.S. became a pawn in the power struggle between Napoleon and Britain. Illegal seizure and condemnation of American vessels and cargo by both sides, mistreatment and impressment of American seamen by the British, and provocative acts like the 1807 attack on the frigate *Chesapeake* by H.M.S. *Leopard* were some of the more obvious results of weak naval strength.

Though ill-prepared, America claimed some naval triumphs in each of its early conflicts with Britain and France. Of special importance was the series of naval victories against the Royal Navy during the War of 1812. Although few in number and of limited strategic importance, these single-ship duels proved that Britannia was not invincible at sea and provided a shot in the arm for American morale. The fleet and squadron battles on the northern lakes in 1813 and 1814 were of greater military value than the single-ship engagements in stemming British offensive power. But in view of the paucity of American land victories naval triumphs, however isolated or limited, were nonetheless a source of genuine pride and hope.

With peace in 1815 came a resurgence of American maritime activity. Whaling voyages, for example, increased in number and duration. The so-called "Golden Age of Whaling" was about to begin.

Undoubtedly some Navy veterans served on board whalers. But even those crewmen who did not see action against the enemy were proud of the showing of the republic's tiny fleet. So when it came to scrimshaw a good many whalemen and other mariners decided to record these notable naval victories on tooth, tusk, and bone.

Of immeasurable help to many scrimshanders was a series of prints and illustrated books detailing key naval engagements. Many engravings and lithographs featured depictions of these battles, a topic that remained popular until eclipsed in the 1860s by more current naval exploits. Books like Abel Bowen's *The Naval Monument* (1816) provided not only fine engraved illustrations but also written descriptions of the incidents.

The popularity of such subjects, even among scrimshanders born twenty years after the events, is remarkable. The fact that Anglo-American relations were not always cordial during the postwar years kept alive memories of 1812. Scrimshanders, like other artists and writers, took endless delight in the game informally known as "pulling the lion's tail." Basically, it consisted of rubbing in the fact that American arms had bested the much-vaunted Royal Navy in fair battle, not once, but repeatedly. "Jonathan," as satirical British writers referred to this upstart nation, was constantly reminding "John Bull" of this embarrassing fact.

The scrimshander's contribution to this game is clearly seen on a number of engraved items, mostly sperm whale teeth. One such example [57] incorporates not one, but two battle scenes on its surface. The front illustrates the moment of surrender of the frigate H.M.S. *Java* to the *Constitution*, December 29, 1812.

After a bloody battle off the coast of Brazil, the American frigate completely dismasted the English ship and so punctured her hull that she subsequently had to be sunk after capture. Without a doubt the scrimshander used an engraving in Bowen's *The Naval Monument* [58] for this effort, to which he added touches of red on the respective flags.

Perhaps the artist was fortunate enough to own a copy of the Bowen book, as he engraved the reverse of this tooth [59] with yet another battle scene from *The Naval Monument* [60]. In April 1814 the American ship-sloop *Peacock* encountered a small British convoy south of Cuba. An eighteen-gun brig, H.M.S. *Epervier,* served as escort. In a battle lasting less than one hour the American ship captured its opponent, which was subsequently added to the U.S. fleet. In depicting the battle the artist followed the Bowen engraving very closely, duplicating with amazing accuracy the fine details of hull, sail, and rigging. He repeated the use of red ink, this time adding it to the gun flashes as well as *Epervier*'s ensign.

The *Constitution* vs. *Java* contest was an especially popular theme because, unlike other defeated British frigates, H.M.S. *Java* was comparable in size and armament, and superior in speed, to her American opposite. Accurate American gunnery seems to have been the telling factor in this victory, and gunnery is stressed in other renderings of this contest. One scrimshander placed these ships on a dark green sea during the early moments of the engagement, when both frigates were largely intact. The outcome of the battle is noted in the engraved legend: "The U.S. Ship of War Constitution Sinking the British Ship Java." An elaborate conglomeration of American patriotic and military devices completes the artist's commemorative effort.

The *Constitution*'s sister ship, the *United States,* took the measure of another of His Majesty's ships, the *Macedonian,* in October 1812. Both frigates were cruising south of the Azores

57. Celebrating an American naval triumph: defeat of H.M.S. *Java* by the frigate *Constitution* in 1812, 6½ in. (16.5 cm.). *Source:* Clarence A. Wimpfheimer, 49.1253

58. Abel Bowen's engraving provided the model for the scrimshander of the *Constitution* vs. *Java* scene. From *The Naval Monument*, 1816.

59. Reverse of the *Constitution* vs. *Java* tooth features the American ship-sloop *Peacock* in battle with H.M.S. *Epervier*, 6½ in. (16.5 cm.). *Source:* Clarence A. Wimpfheimer, 49.1253

60. The inspiration for the *Peacock* vs. *Epervier* rendering was also an Abel Bowen engraving in *The Naval Monument*, 1816.

when the encounter occurred. In 1½ hours the new *Macedonian* had been reduced to a floating hulk by the Yankee. Ironically, among the Britisher's crew were eight impressed American seamen, three of whom were killed by American fire. The five survivors promptly sought their revenge on the English by joining the U.S. Navy.[22]

This was another sweet victory for the Americans, coming as it did in the uncertain early months of the war. An unknown whaleman decided that Bowen's engraving of the scene [61], again from *The Naval Monument,* would do well as a model for his tooth [62]. A thoroughly wrecked *Macedonian* is pictured receiving another devastating broadside from the *United States,* whose only damage appears to be holed sails. Heavy rolling clouds of gunsmoke figure prominently, hiding fully half of the English ship in the process. Again, touches of red ink highlight the scene.

British offensive thrusts from Canada were blunted by hastily built naval squadrons on both Lake Erie and Lake Champlain. Commemorating these signal victories is a phenomenal matched pair of sperm whale teeth [see color plate opp. p. 81] richly colored in blues and red. The heavily engraved scenes of each battle are neatly contained in almost perfectly rectangular fields with the respective titles "BATTLE OF LAKE ERIE,—

61 (top). The frigate *United States* delivers another deadly broadside against a wrecked H.M.S. *Macedonian.* Abel Bowen captured the action in an engraving in his work *The Naval Monument* published in 1816.

62 (center). An unidentified scrimshander's interpretation of Bowen's *United States* vs. *Macedonian* battle scene, 6¼ in. (15.9 cm.). *Source:* Mrs. James H. Stivers, 40.115

63 (bottom). This 1846 N. Currier lithograph provided the image for the impressive Battle of Lake Champlain tooth. See color plate opposite p. 81. *Source:* Harold H. Kynett, 59.1151

PERRY'S VICTORY." and "BATTLE OF LAKE CHAMPLAIN.—
MᶜDONOUGH'S VICTORY." engraved below. A heavily incised
double sawtooth border encircles the butt edge of each tooth.
The reverse sides feature engravings of the appropriate American commanders, Oliver Hazard Perry and Thomas McDonough.

Research indicates that the Lake Champlain battle scene was
inspired by an N. Currier lithograph [63] published in 1846.
What is curious is the fact that this engraved scene is a mirror
image of the print, identical but completely reversed. A similar

64. The hazards of naval service. Top, the crew takes in sail
aboard a storm-tossed naval brig, 5⅞ in. (15.0 cm.). Below,
a hapless warship flanked by two adversaries, 6⅜ in. (16.2 cm.).
Sources: Charles E. White, 39.1777A; Museum purchase, 52.43

65. Symbol of American naval might: a panbone portrait of a
U.S. Navy steam frigate of the Civil War period, 7 x 10½ in.
(17.8 x 26.7 cm.). *Source:* Museum purchase, 52.40

print undoubtedly served as a model for the companion tooth
illustrating Perry's Lake Erie victory of 1813. The heavy use of
color on the teeth was probably suggested by the hand-coloring
on the original prints. Meanwhile, the bust-length portraits of
Perry and McDonough can be traced to published engravings
of the men after portraits by John W. Jarvis (1780-1839).

The teeth are believed to have been brought home by Francis
A. Butts, master of the New Bedford whaling bark *Bramin*.
Butts, who began whaling at the age of seventeen, commanded
the 245-ton *Bramin* during a 3½-year voyage to the Pacific,
arriving home with the teeth in mid-1851. The Currier lithograph was published the year before the *Bramin* voyage and
thus was readily available. What is not known, however, is

whether Butts himself did the engraving or if some other whaleman-artist deserves the credit. What is certain is that these teeth exemplify scrimshaw of the highest quality.

The rigors of seafaring affected warships as much as whaling and other merchant craft. Their crews faced the same dangers from the elements, a fact illustrated on a slightly damaged sperm whale tooth [64]. A scrimshander has engraved a starboard view of a naval brig being tossed about wildly in a squall. Visible clinging to the yards and bowsprit are crewmen attempting to take in sail just as a large wave breaks over the side. There is no way of telling whether the scrimshander was actually on board the vessel or if he created this scene from imagination. The fact remains, though, that he has captured convincingly the age-old drama of men and the sea on this piece.

An interesting and unusual naval scene, visually speaking, is that engraved on a tooth [64] by an unknown whaleman. This is not a single-ship duel, nor is it a fleet action. Rather we see an unidentified warship in the unenviable position of being hemmed in by two opposing vessels of war, and no doubt taking a pasting as a result. The unfortunate in the center is positioned stern to the viewer while the attackers are depicted on converging courses. The heavy gunfire highlighted in red indicates that the battle will probably be a short one.

As the nineteenth century progressed new technological advances changed forever the character of warfare at sea. Chief among these developments was the introduction of steam propulsion. By the 1850s the U.S. Navy had in service a number of large steam frigates and ship-sloops that could operate without complete dependence on the capricious winds and tides. A large steam frigate, perhaps the *Wabash* or one of her sisters, fills a panbone slab [65] measuring 7 by 10½ inches. The vessel is pictured steaming along, all sails furled, with her impressive armament rolled out in plain view. Both the water and the flags are highlighted with blue coloring. An uninked practice sketch of rigging occupies the reverse along with this partially legible pencil notation:

> Made by Leoras [?] . . . of
> Provincetown on board
> Whaleship . . . done with a
> pen knife.

A frustrating coincidence is the fact that the names of both the scrimshander and his whaleship are so marred as to make deciphering virtually impossible. The piece probably dates to the mid-1850s or later, when such steam frigates were the most powerful warships afloat and the pride of the American navy.

Politics and Patriotism

Pride in the young nation's naval exploits was only one expression of the broad wave of patriotic fervor that swept the country after the War of 1812. Many Americans felt that we had at last "paid our dues," and that our existence as a democratic nation had been insured.

Among a people not fully literate, symbols often were more important than the printed word as a medium of popular expression. The flag, certainly, was one such expression; so too were various groupings of flags and military accouterments. But perhaps first and foremost among this national imagery was the bald eagle.

The eagle's adoption as the national symbol followed a frustrating six years of study by committee after committee of the Continental Congress. Once accepted in 1782 as the central element in the national seal, it became rather quickly the most widely recognized emblem of America, both here and abroad.

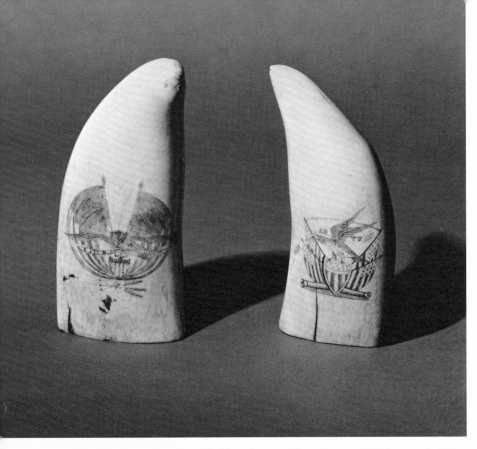

66. The ubiquitous American bald eagle was a favorite patriotic image. At left, a curiously spelled motto, "E PLUR.S UИUM," 6½ in. (16.5 cm). "LIBERTY" is the eagle's message at right, 5¾ in. (14.6 cm). *Sources:* Charles E. White, 39.1785; Mrs. Alexander O. Vietor, 81.64.18

One story has it that an itinerant painter first combined the eagle with arrows, olive branch, and the motto "Federal Union" in decorating a wall of a Washington, Connecticut, house sometime in the 1770s.[23] The motto *E Pluribus Unum,* meaning "one composed of many," was selected in 1776 by one of the committees of Congress charged with designing the Great Seal.[24] Taken from a Latin poem, possibly by Virgil, it soon became the standard message carried on the eagle's scroll banner.

In time the symbol of the bald eagle began to appear as decoration on all types of consumer goods, including those imported from Europe, and even England. The popularity of the image was not lost on British merchants and manufacturers eager to regain lost markets after the Revolution.[25]

Given the fact that a whaleman was as patriotic as the next fellow, and given too the fact that so many articles, including documents, advertisements, and durable goods, carried eagle decoration, it is not surprising that this winged symbol of the new nation turns up on a number of scrimshaw items. The complexity and quality of the engravings vary widely with the skills of the scrimshanders and the style of the model image used.

Eagles of all shapes, sizes, and characters are to be found on decorative scrimshaw in the collection. A fair number of utilitarian items, to be discussed in the following chapter, also share this motif. Sometimes the eagle appeared by itself, unencumbered by other imagery. One tooth in the collection, for example, features the national bird perched on a tree limb. But the bald eagle was oftentimes the central figure in a more complicated scheme. An excellent example of this approach is found in a whale tooth [66] engraved with a patriotic design that includes a pair of American flags, a shield, and a trio of arrows, in addition to the eagle with scroll banner. The scrimshander achieved almost perfect symmetry in his plan, but his spelling leaves something to be desired, as the national motto reads "E PLUR.S UИUM." Red and blue ink highlight appropriate areas of the flags.

Another scrimshander avoided the pitfalls of foreign language completely by labeling a scroll with the word "LIBERTY," certainly a good second choice. Completing the patriotic device engraved on this small sperm whale tooth [66] is the triumphant eagle with shield, flags, and crossed cannons. The martial flavor of this scheme is quite consistent with the engraving of an American frigate on the reverse. Red ink accents portions of both designs.

Thus far we have noted eagles perched in a tree and hovering unaided in midair. One scrimshander decided to provide a more substantial resting place for this feathered symbol of American strength and unity. Thus on a whale tooth [67] we find that ancient structure, the obelisk, transformed into a patriotic monument, complete with timepiece. Atop this stone shaft sits the imperious-looking bird, again with banner and national shield. A trio of U.S. flags on either side of the base flanks the

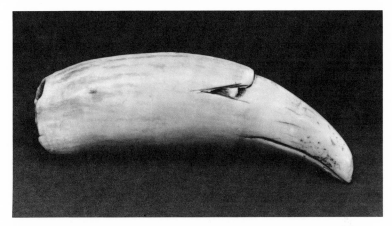

68. "Old Abe" is the name etched on this determined-looking eagle, carved from a small whale tooth, 5 in. (12.7 cm.). *Source:* Mrs. Raynham Townshend, 47.1386

67. A golden patina distinguishes a tooth featuring an American eagle perched atop an obelisk, 5 3/8 in. (13.7 cm.). *Source:* Mrs. Lawrence M. C. Smith, 57.712

monument, itself raised up at least three steps. The significance of the 1:58 reading on the clock is not explained by our anonymous artist.

An unusual treatment of the bald eagle is illustrated by a tooth [68] carved into the shape of the bird's head. The natural curvature of the piece succeeds wonderfully in duplicating the shape of the head and beak. This is not a friendly eagle, but one that communicates strength and wariness. The scrimshander's engraved label, "Old Abe," suggests that the piece might date to the Civil War, symbolizing Union strength and determination.

Eagles were certainly the predominant symbol of America in earlier years, and remain fairly popular today. Those who complain of an overuse of this motif on decorative items, scrimshaw included, should remember that Benjamin Franklin, a persuasive member of the Continental Congress, lobbied for another national symbol—the wild turkey. It is amusing to speculate as to just how many examples of *Meleagris gallapavo* would have been engraved by scrimshanders if the good doctor had had his way.

Perhaps second in popularity to the bald eagle as a patriotic symbol was George Washington. During the early years of the nineteenth century Washington was a symbol of independence, unity, and, perhaps most important, stability. His enduring place in the national fabric was assured even before his death in 1799. Representations of the Virginian were many, and in quality ran the gamut from fine Gilbert Stuart life portraits to almost unrecognizable primitive renderings.

Among the many teeth in the Museum depicting the warrior-statesman is one example [69] illustrating a young blue-jacketed Washington eyeing what appears to be a cherry tree, a bladed implement in his hand. Undoubtedly this engraving was inspired by the cherry tree story concocted by Washington's early biographer, Parson Weems. The Weems tale, though apocryphal, caught the popular imagination and was long accepted as true.

When next we see Washington he is in the role of founding father, dressed in full military regalia. This example [69], the mate to the Napoleon tooth [53] examined earlier, was created by a whaleman whose engraving ability clearly far outstripped his knowledge of spelling or U.S. history. For in Washington's hand is a scroll that reads: "1776/CONSTUTION/July 4th/G Washington." The allegorical figure of "HOPE" on the reverse with her symbolic anchor suggests the possibility that this pair of teeth was made by a Rhode Islander, whose own state's motto is "Hope."

By the beginning of the nineteenth century Washington, no longer a mere mortal, possessed the status of demigod in the national pantheon. As such he was fair game for sculptors of public monuments and the like. An equestrian statue of the man in a park setting is engraved on the side of a sperm whale tooth [69]. The scrimshander achieved an interesting visual effect by "stippling" the entire scene using short incised dashes.

Other figures, too, personified America and its founding principles. The allegorical figure of Liberty was one such early patriotic symbol. Her flag-draped figure graces a small whale tooth [70]. In her right hand she holds a red-striped federal shield and in her left hand is a liberty pole topped with a liberty cap. This specific image is quite popular, as numerous pieces of almost identical design appear in other scrimshaw collections.

Justice was another of the country's guiding precepts that found visual expression in human form and, in turn, on decorative items like scrimshawed teeth. One example [70] depicts the personification of Justice seated and holding her symbols of office, the scales and the sword. Research indicates that, though obviously the work of different hands, this ivory portrait and that of Liberty just mentioned were copied from companion illustrations.[26]

While Liberty and Justice represented characteristics espoused by the nation, America herself was also personified by the heroic female figure of Columbia. A towering symbol often dressed in helmet and classical garb, Columbia expressed a national sense of purpose at once strong and refined. Nearly half of the side of a 28½-inch-long walrus tusk [71] is committed to a spectacular engraving of a statue of this national goddess. For his model the scrimshander had to look no further than the frontispiece of the annual volume of *Harper's Weekly* magazine for the years 1861-1870 [72]. Other patriotic symbols, including eagles and George Washington, accompany Columbia. The

69. George Washington as treated by three different scrimshanders. From left, the boy and the cherry tree, 5½ in. (14.0 cm.); the warrior-statesman, 5¾ in. (14.6 cm.); and the demigod, 3½ in. (8.9 cm.). *Source:* Charles E. White, 39.1791, 39.1798, 39.1720

70. Allegorical figures were popular patriotic symbols in the nineteenth century. At left, a scrimshander's rendering of Justice, 6½ in. (16.5 cm.); right, a boldly inked Liberty graces a whale tooth, 4⅝ in. (11.8 cm.). *Sources:* Clarence A. Wimpfheimer, 49.1247; Charles E. White, 39.1775

engravings of Civil War commanders like General Nathaniel Banks and Commodore Andrew H. Foote found on the tusk date this piece to the mid-1860s or later.

As a symbol of America, Columbia is probably a refinement of an earlier allegorical figure, the Indian maiden.[27] One impressively decorated walrus tusk is topped by a fine engraving of such a figure. Though the artist is unknown, we shall have more to say about the history of this particular piece shortly.

The American Indian figure retained its popularity as a native symbol of America through the nineteenth century. Indians were among the most popular subjects for carved tobacconist figures, for example. A very similar figure, complete with pipe and tobacco leaves, was transferred onto a whale tooth [73] by an unknown scrimshander. Pin pricks indicate that the figure was copied from a full-size published illustration, perhaps a tobacco advertisement. The artist probably relied on his own skill to provide the landscape in the background.

Symbolic of the meeting of Old World and New is the vignette engraved on a sperm whale tooth [73]. A pair of native Americans, one armed with a war club or musket, stand on the

71 (left). Columbia symbolized the American self-image of strength and dignity. Detail from a walrus tusk. *Source:* Mrs. Lawrence M. C. Smith, 57.702

72 (right). Frontispiece from the annual volumes of *Harper's Weekly* for the decade 1861-1870 provided inspiration for the engraver of the tusk in Figure 71.

PLATE 1: An active volcano dominates this superbly engraved panbone whaling scene.
4³/₈ x 8³/₈ in. (11.1 x 21.3 cm.). *Source:* Harold H. Kynett, 41.448

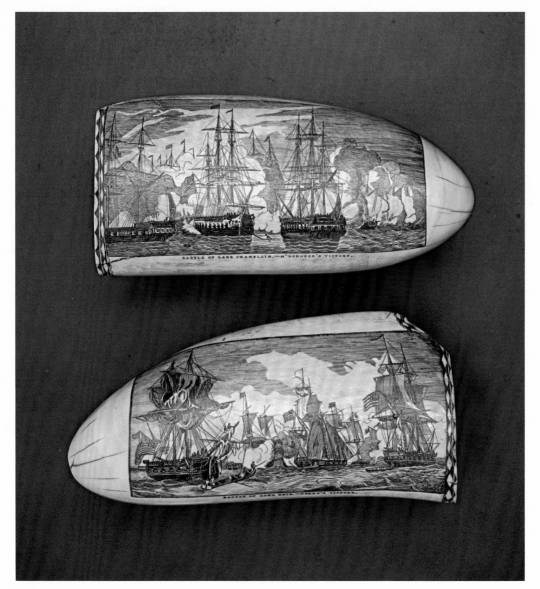

PLATE II: Above, War of 1812 naval battles on Lake Champlain and Lake Erie are commemorated on matched pair of whale teeth, c. 1850, 7½ in. (19.0 cm.). *Source:* Harold H. Kynett, 41.412, 41.411. Right, patriotic sentiment is strong on a whale tooth honoring soldier-statesman Zachary Taylor, 5⅛ in. (13.0 cm.). *Source:* Mrs. Raynham Townshend, 47.1357

shore alongside an anchor and American shield. Completing the scene, perhaps inspired by a map cartouche, is the ubiquitous bald eagle with decorative banner. A touch of color is supplied by the red rose and green leaves at the tip of the tooth.

Zachary Taylor, like Washington, was another soldier turned statesman, serving as the twelfth president. Active in early Indian wars, Taylor reached the pinnacle of his military career during the Mexican War, 1846-1848. Elected chief executive on the Whig ticket in 1848, Taylor served less than half his term, dying of cholera in 1850.

The engraver of one sperm whale tooth [see color plate opposite] was clearly a Taylor supporter, given the amount of effort put into the piece. An excellent profile of Taylor's head is encircled by a laurel wreath and surmounted by the national eagle, complete with banner scroll reading "HONOUR THE BRAVE." Swords and bayonets accompany the engraving, and an elaborate scalloped border of bunting surrounds the base of the tooth. The martial character of the reverse side, with its cannons, drums, and cannon balls, suggests that this piece celebrates Taylor the general rather than Taylor the president. It could, however, conceivably date to 1848, the year that saw the end of the Mexican War and the presidential campaign; and as such the tooth could then be considered a type of political advertisement. Whatever its intended use this tooth, with its tiny drilled holes to highlight detail and its lavishly colored flags and foliage, is a superb example of the scrimshander's art.

A phenomenal matched pair of twenty-five-inch-long walrus tusks [74] carry the political and patriotic theme to an extreme. So many and varied are the individual engravings that it can truthfully be said that there is something here for everyone. One tusk boasts not one but two different American eagles, two renderings of the goddess of Liberty, with what appears to be one of Columbia tossed in for good measure. But Civil War

73. The American Indian as a popular symbol: left, a pin-pricked portrait, possibly from a tobacco advertisement, 6 in. (15.2 cm.); at right, in company with patriotic and nautical devices, 6¼ in. (15.9 cm.). *Sources:* Charles E. White, 39.1800; Mrs. Lawrence M. C. Smith, 57.709

themes predominate in the form of exquisite engravings of generals Sherman and Grant. A very curious element is an etching of two angels, their wings made of U. S. flags, kissing in midair. As the angels are labeled "NORTH" and "SOUTH," the theme of postwar reconciliation is clear.

The mate is also engraved with a bewildering cast of American characters. The Indian maiden already mentioned is accompanied by an eagle with shield, a U. S. flag, a dual portrait of Lincoln and Washington, and a large rendering of Columbia striding briskly toward the viewer. A portrait of Winfield Scott, the venerable commander of the American army when war

74. Patriotic imagery abounds on this matched pair of walrus tusks, which date to the period immediately after the Civil War, 24⅝ in. (62.5 cm.). In the photograph on the opposite page, the tusks are seen flanking the bar mirror. *Source:* Mrs. Lawrence M. C. Smith, 57.705, 57.704

broke out in 1861, is also included. Last but by no means least is a vignette showing three walruses, who in no small way made this and many other scrimshaw items possible. The pair of tusks display appropriate use of red and blue ink, as well as elaborate diamond banding around the bases.

Documenting the history of a scrimshaw piece is no easy task and usually all but impossible. In the case of these tusks, however, an absolutely astounding bit of evidence exists to account for a part of their past.

Following the California gold rush one Abe Warner erected a saloon in San Francisco called the Cobweb Palace, so named because the eccentric proprietor felt that spiders and other indigenous fauna had as much right in the saloon as paying customers.[28] Needless to say, a certain dustiness must have permeated this aptly named watering hole.

The Cobweb Palace thrived in the years that followed and became popular with the increasing numbers of whalemen who called San Francisco home. Now seamen were notoriously short on hard cash, and so Warner took, among other things, scrimshaw in payment for food and a variety of "spiritous liquors." In doing so he amassed a sizable scrimshaw collection, seen flanking the bar mirror in this post Civil War photograph [75]. And among the pieces visible are the pair of patriotic walrus tusks just described. Under close scrutiny the photograph also reveals the matched pair of whale teeth [56] that caricatured both the Chinese and the bloomer fashion.

75. The Cobweb Palace, a famous San Francisco saloon, was frequented by whalemen and mariners. Behind Abe Warner, the proprietor, is a collection of scrimshaw including the two patriotic walrus tusks illustrated in Figure 74. California Historical Society, San Francisco.

Other Motifs

The range of subjects applicable to decorative scrimshaw was limited only by the imagination of the practitioner. The several motifs examined thus far, while perhaps the most prevalent in the Museum collection, are by no means the only ones selected by scrimshanders.

For example, until displaced by the sudden popularity of patriotic and naval imagery following the War of 1812, the theme of nature was addressed by many scrimshanders in their work. One of an unsigned and undated matched pair of whale teeth [76] illustrates this subject quite well. The green and white blossoming tree on the tooth was obviously etched freehand, possibly from the scrimshander's memory of the dogwoods of New England. Stipple engraving of the ground works well in setting off the tree in the scene.

Details of nature also appear on decorative scrimshaw, for instance, the engraving of a flowering twig found on a heavily inked sperm whale tooth [76]. So carefully executed is this piece that it is virtually impossible to tell whether the scrimshander used a printed illustration or a real twig as his model. It is only regrettable that the artist did not have the appropriate colors to add to his botanical illustration.

Another motif which appears on scrimshaw, often in conjunction with other subjects, is that of geometric patterns. While many busks, ditty boxes, and other utilitarian pieces

76. The theme of nature as addressed by two unidentified scrimshanders: at left, a free-handed flowering tree, 5 in. (12.7 cm.); right, a flowering twig, possibly detailed from an actual specimen, 6½ in. (16.5 cm.). *Sources:* Estate of Bradley H. Barnes, 73.423; Charles E. White, 39.1739

or two of these designs are found on a piece, but in the case of one tooth [77] fully one entire side is devoted to these fraternal images. The artist was certainly proud of his work, as he engraved his name, Henry R. Abbott, in bold shaded letters. Surrounding the name is a collection of Masonic symbols, including hammer, trowel, level, square and compass, Jacob's ladder, and Solomon's Seal. A double topsail bark and the notation "BOSTON/1866/HA" occupy the reverse. The Boston city directory of 1866 lists a Henry R. Abbott, though his occupation is the landbound one of clerk. Whether this is the same Abbott or not and, if so, whether he ever spent time at sea has yet to be learned. Nonetheless the piece remains an excellent example of Masonic scrimshaw decoration.

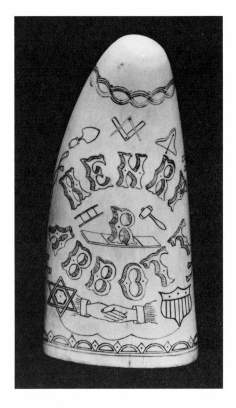

77. Henry R. Abbott covered this tooth with Masonic emblems in 1866, 5¼ in. (13.4 cm.). *Source:* Anonymous, 70.317

display such decoration, its use on purely decorative items is most often found in intricate border designs surrounding vignettes or encircling the base edges of teeth and tusks. Some scrimshanders, however, worked these patterns into the scenes themselves, for example the crosshatched flooring under the fashionable woman encountered on a previous example [44].

A more ambitious undertaking is that of the young woman engraved on a whale tooth [45] noted earlier in this chapter. Her dress is one great collection of squares and diamonds formed from intersecting lines. The woman was copied from an illustration, but the decorative details are most likely the scrimshander's own.

Masonic symbols occasionally appear on scrimshaw, often together with patriotic or nautical emblems. Normally only one

Chapter 4 *Functional Forms: Utilitarian Scrimshaw*

THE scrimshander's primary raw materials, notably ivory, whalebone, and baleen, lent themselves to conversion into articles of everyday use. Ivory's fine, hard grain, whalebone's useful size and strength, and baleen's resiliency led to their widespread employment in a variety of applications. In many of these utilitarian objects mechanical craftsmanship is complemented by artistry equal to that found on purely decorative work.

Fashion accessories and articles for kitchen use are two of the better-known classifications into which utilitarian scrimshaw can be divided. We will examine objects in these and other categories, their construction, decoration, and uses.

Clothing Accessories

Busks are among the better-known utilitarian items produced by the whaleman. Ranging from 8 to 14 inches in length and averaging approximately 1½ inches in width, these tongue-depresser-shaped slabs were designed for use as the front stay of a woman's corset, and as such contributed to the narrow waist style common to women's fashions from at least the sixteenth through the nineteenth centuries.

It is believed that busks date far into antiquity, perhaps from as early as 500 B.C., when both men and women used them.[1] Fashion changes in the nineteenth century reduced the busk's importance as a clothing accessory, though its use lingered in some cases. But while there is no doubt that scrimshaw busks were often intended primarily as keepsakes or mementos, their original function was not completely forgotten either; a fact testified to by one whaleman's inscription:

> Accept, dear Girl this busk from me;
>   Carved by my humble hand.
> I took it from a Sparm Whale's Jaw,
>   One thousand miles from land!
> In many a gale
> Has been the Whale,
>   In which this bone did rest,
> His time is past,
> His bone at last
>   Must now support thy brest.[2]

As intimated by this anonymous whaleman-bard, panbone from the sperm whale's jaw was widely used in the creation of corset busks. Panbone's straight grain and its ability to be cut and planed down to the ⅛ inch thickness required for these stays contributed to its popularity as a raw material. Likewise was baleen, erroneously termed "whalebone" in the nineteenth century, employed in many busks, sharing as it did most of the qualities of panbone.

Add to this the fact that, unlike with other utilitarian items, great mechanical skill was not required to make a busk, and you have one explanation for the popularity of this item among scrimshanders.[3] Further, the flat bone or baleen surface was ideal for engraving. Certainly it was easier to incise than the curving surface of a tooth, and on the whole offered more usable area for decoration.

Wives and sweethearts were the usual recipients of scrimshaw busks. Sometimes the incised decoration was randomly chosen and without special significance, but in other cases the scrimshander personalized the piece with engravings of particular people, places, or events.

Many of the etched motifs were similar to those applied to decorative pieces like teeth and tusks. Of these themes perhaps the most popular were home, geometric patterns, and nature symbols. Whaling and naval scenes and patriotic imagery are less frequently encountered.

78. Busks provided a perfect surface for elaborate engraving. From left, a baleen busk initialed "M.S.H." displays various nature images, 13 11/16 in. (34.8 cm.); whalebone busk dated 1842 includes a woman's portrait and hearts, 13 9/16 in. (34.4 cm.); heavily inked busk of whalebone surrounds naval vignette with floral displays, 14 3/16 in. (36.0 cm.). *Sources:* Charles E. White, 39.1912; Dr. Charles K. Stillman, 36.80; Harold H. Kynett, 41.613

A fine introduction to the scrimshaw busk is provided by an example [78] made of baleen. The decoration includes a five-pointed star with elaborately incised concentric circles, a classical urn and small basket or pot, each filled with flowers, a two-story frame house, and a heart-within-a-heart motif at the very top. As with other busks the top of this piece is rounded and lobed, defining the top of the heart. Several other geometric and natural elements, including an encircling vinework border, complete this busk, which bears the script initials "M. S. H."

A whalebone busk [78] dated 1842 combines sentiment with geometric and natural motifs. A woman's portrait framed by a window occupies the uppermost position on this work. That she is most likely the whaleman's wife or lady love is suggested by the pair of lovebirds and four red inked hearts engraved

toward the bottom of the busk. Sunbursts, rosettes, an urn with flowers, and other imagery complete this fine effort.

Heavy use of color characterizes a whalebone busk [78], which, though largely decorated with floral designs, includes a port view of an American warship at anchor. Almost the entire surface of the busk is inked in red, green, black, or sepia, and it reflects well the skill of the scrimshander.

If the date 1769 engraved on a baleen busk [79] in the collection is genuine, then this object ranks among the earliest of dated scrimshaw pieces. Here geometry and sentimentality combine in the form of interlocking hearts. A rosette within a striped border, wreath work, and a multistory neoclassical building complete the decoration. The scrimshander in this case

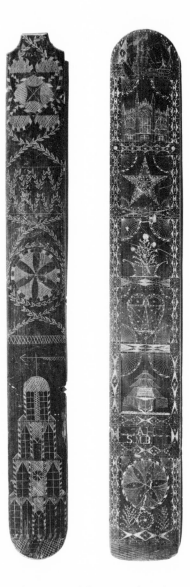

79. Baleen was a plentiful material for scrimshaw items. Left, a finely etched busk dated 1769, 13¼ in. (33.7 cm.); and right, an exquisite busk made by Albert Harris for his wife, 13⅜ in. (34.0 cm.). *Sources:* A. D. Akin, 50.316; New England Savings Bank, 39.883

opted for a short tab rather than curved lobes at the top of the busk.

Only a few of the Museum's busks carry the identity of the maker or recipient. One of these examples [79], made of baleen, has an almost overwhelming concentration of incised decoration, which includes, besides familiar geometric and nature imagery, a very unusual stern view of a ship with all studding sails set. Below this nautical vignette are the initials "A. H./S. M. B." The clue to the whaleman's identity is found in a barely legible and previously overlooked inscription etched on the reverse, which reads: "A presant from my husband. Charlotte M. Harris . . . ." Therefore "A. H." must be "A. Harris"; but "S. M. B." is confusing until one considers the variant spelling of Charlotte as "Sharlotte." "S. M. B." were quite possibly the initials of Mrs. Harris's maiden name, which in turn suggests that the busk was done before their marriage, and the inscription on the reverse added later.

Another, unfinished busk in the Seaport collection bears the initials "A H" and the name "Albert Harris" lightly scratched on the reverse. The lettering style suggests that this was almost certainly Charlotte's whaleman husband.

A trio of whalebone busks [80], though each of different size, shape, and engraving style, share an unusual trait. Etched on each of these pieces is a depiction of a balloon ascension, a popular nineteenth-century spectacle, and certainly one far removed from the whaleman's normal experience. A pair of the balloons fly flags from the gondolas, and two of these lighter-than-air craft incorporate a parachute arrangement between gas bag and gondola, perhaps as a safety measure against the possibility of problems aloft. The smallest of the three stays is marked "Rachael" and dated 1833, while the others, largely geometric in decoration, lack any identification.

One of the myths surrounding scrimshaw is that it was only done on board whalers. Another misconception is the belief that men alone practiced the art. A fine baleen busk [81] in the Museum's collection proves both of these assumptions to be incorrect. The busk combines familiar imagery like a five-pointed star within a circle, a flower urn, and heavy wreath decoration along borders and between scenes. At the bottom is the inscription "MRS. MARY E. STARK/On Board the Ship B. F./Hoxie."

Mary E. Rathbun Stark (1826-1909) of Mystic was the wife of Captain Henry S. Stark, master of the Mystic-built clipper *B. F. Hoxie*, completed in 1855. Mrs. Stark accompanied her husband on the first voyage of the ship, from Philadelphia to San Francisco, thence to Honolulu, and finally back to New York. A series of marvelous letters written during the voyage by Mrs. Stark to her daughter Lizzie are in the collection of the Seaport's G. W. Blunt White Library and cover the nine months from April 1855 to January 1856.[4]

From these letters certain information concerning the busk can be gleaned. For instance, it was a lack of return cargo in San Francisco that brought the 1387-ton *B. F. Hoxie* to Honolulu. There a good quantity of whaling products were found to fill the hold, including eight thousand barrels of whale oil. A more relevant portion of the cargo for our purposes was the 125 *tons* of

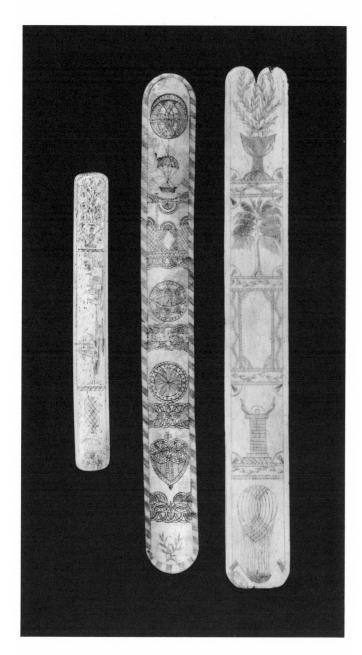

80. Whalebone busks and hot air balloons: left to right, a small example dated 1833, 8¹/₁₆ in. (20.5 cm.); rosettes and other geometric designs dominate an intricately detailed busk, 13⁷/₁₆ in. (34.2 cm.); plant life and a lighthouse accompany a balloon on a large busk, 14 in. (35.5 cm.). *Sources:* Charles E. White, 39.1910; Dr. Charles K. Stillman, 36.79; Charles E. White, 39.1907

81. Mystic's Mary E. Stark proved that not all scrimshanders were whalemen. Note the quality of the engraving on this baleen busk, 14⁹/₁₆ in. (37.0 cm.). *Source:* Miss Julia Randall, 48.1043

82. Panoramic views on whalebone busks: top, a busy landlocked harbor scene, 13⁵/16 in.
(33.8 cm.); below, heavily stylized water distinguishes another whalebone busk, 13¹/8 in. (33.3 cm.).
Sources: Dr. Ier J. Manwaring, 59.1134; Mrs. Alexander O. Vietor, 81.64.24

baleen shipped, so much that even part of the woman's cabin was filled with this material. This clearly explains Mrs. Stark's acquisition of baleen.

Another piece of the story is offered by Captain Stark who, in writing from Honolulu to his father in Mystic, noted: "I think we have got a good crew now, mostly whalemen."⁵ With a ship full of baleen, a crew composed largely of whalemen, and some long months ahead of her, it is no wonder that Mary Stark tried her hand at scrimshaw, probably with some guidance from one of the crew. Her own beautiful handwriting and the fact that she carried along a good deal of sewing gear, including fine needles, undoubtedly contributed to the high quality of her finished product, which, incidentally, also includes a detail of the *Hoxie's*

rigging and several buildings. In all, a fine piece of work by a most talented artist.

A variation of the familiar multiple vignette style of engraving is illustrated on a number of busks in the Seaport. In several cases a single horizontal panoramic scene is incised, the end product resembling an elongated panbone plaque. On one such example [82] a busy harbor filled with sloops and schooners is flanked by twin villages with closely packed buildings. American flags fly from one of the structures and several vessels in the harbor. A schooner or hermaphrodite brig flies what could possibly be the striped ensign of the Hawaiian Islands, not an unreasonable guess given the tropical foliage present. The unexplained inclusion of oversize flowerpots lends a toylike appearance to the entire scene. The artist used green, blue, and red ink to highlight appropriate areas of this interesting panorama.

Most busks are decorated on one side only, though several in the Museum carry engraving on both front and back. One of these, a handsome whalebone specimen [82], displays a sweeping scene centering on a hilly island, complete with town and snug harbor. Several full-rigged ships are included, as is a headland with lighthouse at the extreme left.

Not satisfied with this much work, or perhaps short on materials, the scrimshander turned his attention to the reverse of the piece and engraved a splendid harbor scene. Whether this port, with its variety of shipping, is the same as pictured on the front is uncertain. One possibility is that the front of the busk depicts a distant whaling ground, and the reverse scene is the whaleman's image of home.

Whereas the busk was almost always made as a gift for wife or girl friend, the cane was normally an item that the scrimshander crafted for himself. Canes were an important part of a gentleman's dress in the nineteenth century, and even whalemen and sailors might observe this fashion when ashore. Thus did a bored boatsteerer aboard the whaleship *Clifford Wayne* record in his diary in 1844: "Nothing to do but make canes to support our dignity when we are home."[6]

Unlike purely decorative pieces, or even busks, canes demanded a bit of craftsmanship to produce. One of the most popular materials was whalebone, usually from the jaw of the sperm whale, which was cut into long rectangular sticks and then laboriously filed or, more rarely, turned on a lathe to achieve the rounded shaft. Woods of various types were also employed in this way in lieu of whalebone. Shafts might be completely round, or portions of them could be octagonal or hexagonal in section. Inlays of ivory, wood, baleen, mother-of-pearl, and other materials are also found.

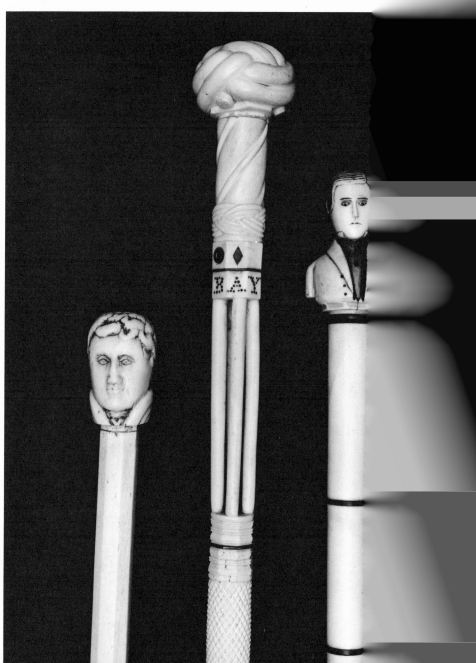

83. A pair of likelike ivory heads flank a carved ivory Turk's-head knot on scrimshaw canes. The cane at center is marked "C. BAYLEY" with tiny inlaid brads. *Sources:* Charles E. White, 39.1842; Harold H. Kynett, 41.370, 41.394

Often the head of the cane was of whale or walrus ivory, and usually carved, filed, turned, or engraved in some specific manner. This is the portion that gave each cane its distinctive character and, literally, its "feel." As such it often exhibited creativity of a high order on the part of the scrimshander.

Some of the engraved motifs used on decorative items became three-dimensional when applied to the construction of these walking sticks. For example, geometric patterns took on depth when carved on whalebone or ivory shafts. Spiral turning of cane shafts to resemble rope is just one of these treatments used on several of the Seaport's canes. Some of these in turn are topped by an ivory head carved in the popular Turk's-head knot motif.

This turban-shaped rope design is used on the head of an elaborate cane [83] that includes spiral turning along a portion of the whalebone shaft. A variety of inlays, including tortoiseshell, ivory, and bronze, add color and texture to the piece. One section uses an unusual four-column design topped by the name "C. BAYLEY" inlaid in tiny brads. There is a possibility that this is Charles Bayley, in 1868 a thirty-one-year-old crewman aboard the bark *Roman* of New Bedford.

Carved portraits appear on several walking sticks. The first of these [83] has a turned whalebone shaft hexagonal in section just below the cane head. The ivory handle is carved in the shape of a man's head, with a high starched collar evident.

Another cane [83] sports a bust-length portrait of an unidentified gentleman. The character's bearing resembles that of a figurehead carving, and his hair and clothing are well inked in black. A composite shaft of wood and whale ivory with baleen disk insets completes the piece.

A curious motif is that of a delicately carved woman's leg, bent ninety degrees at the knee to form a functional handle. This cane [84] with its whalebone shaft has additional decora-

tion in the form of two rings of baleen at the junction of shaft and handle. A third tiny ring encircles the ankle. Some feel this motif reflects repressed sexual feelings on the part of the scrimshander, a type of expression that did not appear frequently on decorative pieces.

Repressed emotions of another kind are attributed to the clenched fist design found on quite a few scrimshaw canes. A number of the walking sticks in the Museum carry this symbol, which some believe represents pent-up male rage resulting from the inherent and seemingly contradictory pressures of shipboard isolation and overcrowding. Certainly such a hefty item as a cane could become a dangerous weapon in the wrong hands. A less bellicose explanation holds that the fist illustrates

84. Both of these ivory cane head designs are thought to represent repressed sexual feelings among shipbound whalemen. *Sources:* Harold H. Kynett, 41.361; Mrs. Raynham Townshend, 47.1336

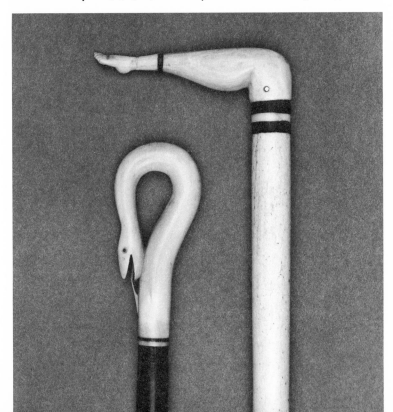

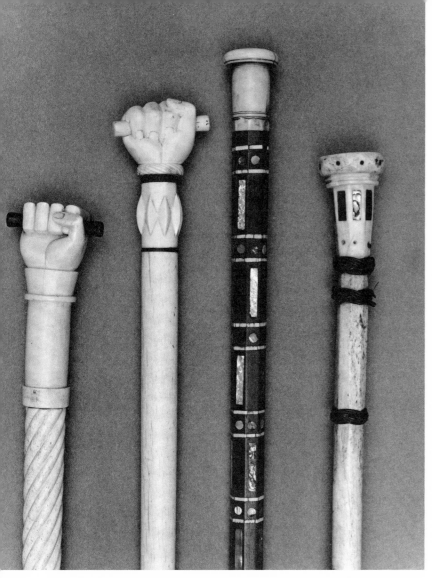

85. The fist motif appears on a number of scrimshaw canes and is believed to be an expression of frustration and anger. Other canes are distinguished by elaborate inlays of ivory, baleen, and shell. *Sources:* Harold H. Kynett, 41.360; Charles E. White, 39.1836; Mrs. James H. Stivers, 40.119; Anonymous, 70.690

the method of holding or using the piece, though this, too, is speculative.

One of our canes [85] is composed of a rope twist whalebone shaft with a decorative rope band in the middle. The square, carved fist holds what appears to be a wooden peg. Another piece [85] has a much less stylized hand, this time clasping an ivory stick nearly identical to the piece of wood found in the preceding cane. An elaborate carved cuff section includes eight raised diamonds with flanking rings of baleen.

Coiled serpents appear on some cane heads and this motif, too, has been described as sexual in nature. One particular example [84], made of ivory, is carved in a loop, providing not only an unusual decorative effect, but also a means of grasping

86. The American bald eagle motif was not restricted to purely decorative items alone. *Sources:* Harold H. Kynett, 41.384; Charles E. White, 39.1846

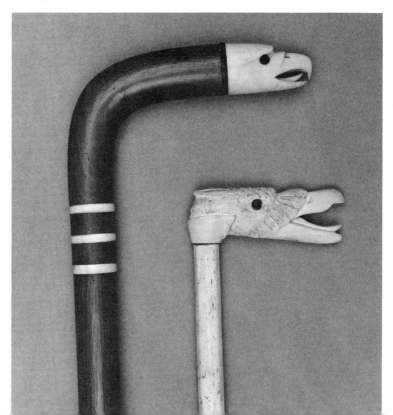

or hanging the stick. Bands of baleen and ivory separate the ivory head from the wooden shaft.

The popular symbol of American independence, the eagle, was utilized in canes as well as in decorative scrimshaw items. A particularly fierce-looking ivory bird caps a whalebone cane [86]. The raptor's no-nonsense look and gaping beak suggest hostility or wariness. Its beady eyes are just that—two tiny amber glass beads. Like other walking sticks in the collection, this piece has a metal ferrule tip to prevent undue wear or damage to the bone shaft.

Another cane [86] topped by our feathered national symbol is composed largely of wood, not bone. A trio of ivory rings at the neck of the cane adds the only other contrasting decoration besides the ivory head itself. This ivory bird is somewhat less threatening in appearance than that on the head of the previous cane, and has eyes composed of wood and baleen.

Inlays of certain materials figure prominently in the decoration of many scrimshaw canes. One piece [85] with bone shaft and ivory head is inlaid with eight alternating strips of tortoiseshell and abalone. Heads of small nails used in attaching the shaft and handle also serve as decoration. The flat top of the cane handle is further inlaid with a large iridescent abalone disk, while four woven reed bands complete the decoration on the tapering shaft.

Spectacular inlays characterize a hardwood and ivory walking stick [85] whose shaft, like others in the collection, is basically octagonal in section, becoming round as it tapers at the tip. Seven pairs of narrow ivory bands plus one larger ring divide the upper half of the cane. The intervening segments are further adorned with variously shaped inlays of mother-of-pearl. An ivory handle caps this impressive scrimshaw effort.

Inlay provides a bit of documentation for a wooden cane [87] that has an ivory ferrule tip in addition to the more usual

ivory head. While the shaft has two handsome inlaid diamonds of ivory, the real story is the handle, which, curiously, is carved in the shape of a barrel. The barrel heads are both inlaid, one with mother-of-pearl, the other with an 1845 Chilean coin. The coin indicates that the piece was made no earlier than 1845, and further suggests that it was made on a Pacific whaling cruise. Valparaiso, Chile's major seaport, was a frequent port of call for Yankee whalers voyaging to and from the Pacific.

An example of utilitarian scrimshaw produced by naval personnel is the walking stick [88] created by William S. Somerby, a sailmaker aboard the frigate *Constitution*. The piece consists of an ivory knob and a two-piece whalebone shaft, all separated by

87. An 1845 Chilean coin, possibly acquired by a whaleman during shore leave in Valparaiso, is inlaid in this barrel-shaped ivory cane head. Captain James Earle's ivory-headed walking stick dates to 1902. *Sources:* Mrs. James H. Stivers, 40.118; Museum purchase, 78.253

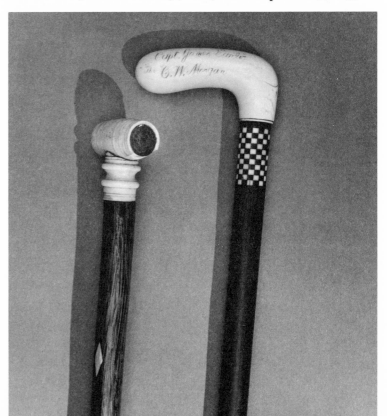

88. William S. Somerby, a sailmaker aboard the U.S.S. *Constitution,* recorded the ship's journeys during the years 1839-1841. *Source:* Harold H. Kynett, 41.367

silver bands. The octagonal top segment of the cane chronicles part of that frigate's service upon being dispatched to the Pacific as flagship of the South Pacific squadron.[7] Somerby's cane records the following data:

U. S. CONSTITUTION. CAPTAIN DANIEL TURNER
BEARING THE BROAD PENNANT OF COMMODORE ALEX.
    CLAXTON
NORFOLK MARCH 1, 1839. NEW YORK APRIL 25 VERACRUZ
    MAY 18.
HAVANNA JULY 4 RIO JANIERO SEPT 1. VALPARAISO NOV. 2
CALLAO JAN. 1 1840 TALCUHUANA MARCH 15. PAYTA MAY 11.
PUNA SEPT. 20. JUAN FERNANDEZ. JULY 24. 1841.
WILLIAM S. SOMERBY

Of particular interest to the Museum is a handsome wooden walking stick [87]. Engraved on the whale ivory handle is the following: "Capt. James Earle/The C. W. Morgan/1902." Cap-

tain Earle commanded the *Charles W. Morgan* for a total of eight voyages during the periods 1891-1896 and 1900-1908. For most of this time the bark sailed from San Francisco, not returning to New Bedford until 1906, after some twenty years absence. It is not known whether Captain Earle's cane, with its intricate checkerboard inlay of ivory, was made by him or by some other individual. It is, however, the only piece in the scrimshaw collection directly related to the Museum's venerable vessel.

Before leaving the subject of canes, it should be mentioned that whalemen sometimes used the backbones of sharks in the construction of walking sticks. Sharks were often present, especially during the bloody cutting-in process. Whalemen would frequently kill these feared predators, and occasionally their hollow disklike vertebrae would be strung over a metal rod, forming a sturdy walking stick. Illustrating the end product of such activity is a shark vertebra cane [89] some thirty-four

89. Baleen disks accent this shark vertebra cane, the handiwork of an unidentified whaleman, 34 in. (86.4 cm.). *Source:* Earl H. Croft, 53.3590

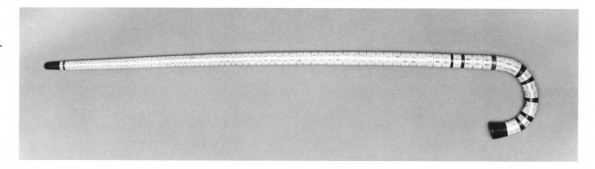

90. Husband and wife scrimshanders: ambrotypes of Captain Frederick H. Smith and Sarah G. "Sallie" Smith. Captain Smith's photograph dates to the Civil War. *Source:* Harold H. Kynett, 41.294

91. Sallie Smith probably decorated this fan while Fred Smith almost certainly produced its turned ivory handle, 14 3/8 in. (36.5 cm.). *Source:* Harold H. Kynett, 41.296

inches in length. Nine bands of variously colored baleen serve as decorations on this, one of several similar pieces in the Museum.

The fan was a popular accessory carried by women in the last century. Its association with scrimshaw is admittedly tenuous, but one fan in the collection claims strong connections to this marine art. Sarah G. "Sallie" Smith accompanied her husband, Captain Frederick H. Smith [90], on voyages aboard several New Bedford whalers, including the *Ohio* and *John P. West*, during the 1870s and 1880s. As noted in Chapter 1, Fred Smith was a prolific scrimshander,[8] aided in no small measure by a portable lathe he reportedly kept in his cabin.

This fan [91], with its circular linen cover, uses a turned piece of whale ivory, most likely fashioned by Captain Smith, as a handle. A turned whalebone shaft supports the fan from the

back. The initial "s" and encircling floral decoration, all hand-painted, are quite likely Sallie's handiwork.

Sallie tried to busy herself with knitting and sewing during the *Ohio*'s 1875-1878 Atlantic cruise. Her diary of the voyage,[9] in the collection of our G. W. Blunt White Library, records the knitting of several shawls. Captain Smith, meanwhile, continued to produce all manner of scrimshaw items, including two shawl clips [92]. Each clip, about three inches long, consists of two overlapping rectangular pieces of ivory with beveled edges. One slab is white while the other has been converted to what Sallie called "nitrated bone," through treatment with a special solution. The resulting burnished effect resembles tarnished silver. When the slabs are assembled and metal pins attached, these clips become as functional as they are handsome.

Scrimshaw jewelry was not a particularly popular item

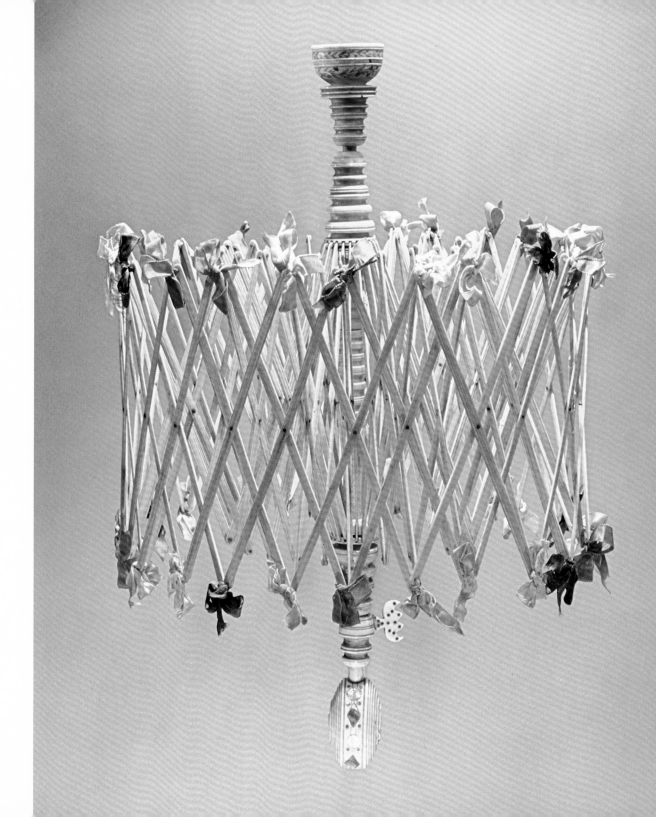

PLATE III: Abalone inlay accents
the base of an ivory and whalebone
scrimshaw swift, 18½ in. (47.0
cm.). *Source:* Mrs. Edward G.
Hammond, 41.22

PLATE IV: Captain John Stivers constructed this box of abalone, ivory, and baleen, possibly as early as 1860, 10$\frac{1}{8}$ x 7$\frac{1}{8}$ in. (25.7 x 18.1 cm.). *Source:* Mrs. James H. Stivers, 40.108

92. Ivory shawl clips made by Fred Smith. The dark slabs are treated to simulate tarnished silver, and inlaid disks of wood hide metal fastenings, 2⅞ in. (7.3 cm.). *Source:* Harold H. Kynett, 41.631.10, 41.631.11

among whalemen. Most of our examples are rings made of whalebone or ivory. One piece [93], carved of whalebone, displays a triumphant American eagle on the face and two unfinished national shields on the sloping sides. Clever use of colored sealing waxes distinguishes another whalebone ring [93] whose red and blue inlays are flanked by completed American shields. Both of these pieces are clearly masculine in appearance and were probably made by scrimshanders for their own use.

93. Scrimshaw jewelry: from left, ivory and wood ring box, 1½ in. (3.8 cm.); ivory ring with wax inlay, ¹⁵/₁₆ in. (2.3 cm.); whalebone ring with engraved American eagle, 1 in. (2.5 cm.); and ivory ring carved with a stylized floral motif, 1 in. (2.5 cm.). *Sources:* Miss Martha Gold Cornell, 58.745; Clarence A. Wimpfheimer, 49.1254; Charles E. White, 39.2026; Mrs. W. A. Wilcox, 63.205

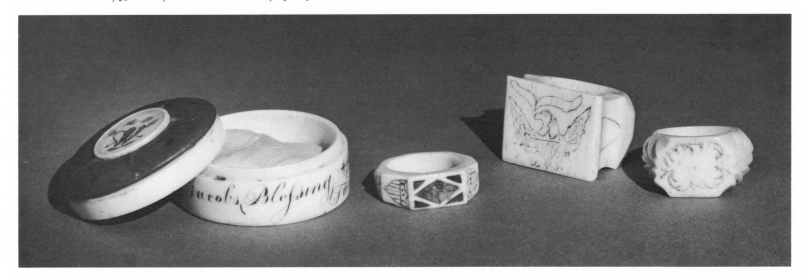

One ivory ring [93] has a more feminine appearance in the intricate, stylized leaf designs carved on the face and sides of the piece. A delicate and unusual item is an ivory and wood ring box [93] measuring 1½ inches in diameter. The wooden lid is inlaid with an ivory disk engraved with interlocking, pierced hearts, and is itself the center of a five-pointed star design. An engraved house with trees on the side is accompanied by the following inscription: "Jacobs Blessing Attend you & Your/Family." The box is believed to have been a gift from a Scottish seaman to a young woman sometime in the 1850s or 1860s.

Sewing Items

Sallie Smith's constant remarks about sewing, knitting, "croshaying," and related needlework were not unusual at a time when most clothing and sewn items were made at home. The many implements required in sewing provided plenty of ideas and opportunities for dexterous scrimshanders anxious to keep busy and at the same time produce something useful. Sallie was fortunate enough to be with her scrimshander-husband, who thus knew exactly what his wife most desired and needed for her constant sewing work. Other whalemen had to guess what items their wives or sweethearts might most appreciate. Thus it is that scrimshaw sewing utensils ranged from the simplest of bodkins to that most intricate of yarn winders, the swift.

Let's begin with one of the more common sewing items, the bodkin. Made of whalebone or ivory, these three-to-six-inch-long stilettos were used for a variety of purposes, including piercing holes in cloth and pulling tapes or ribbons through loops or hems. Women could also use bodkins, especially the very ornate examples, as hair ornaments.

A crude bone example [94] illustrates the basic, unadorned

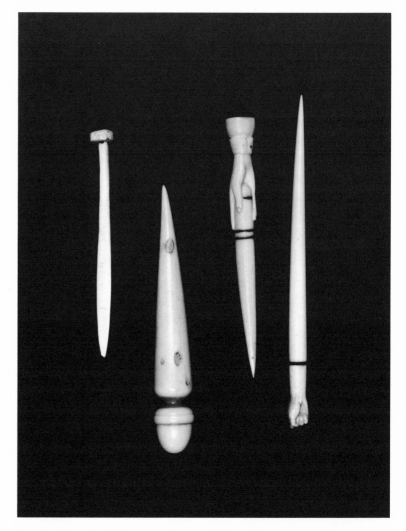

94. Bodkins in all shapes and sizes: left to right, the basic bone implement, 3½ in. (8.9 cm.); ivory piece with acorn decoration, 4⅛ in. (10.5 cm.); ivory bodkin with lifelike hand and red wax inlay, 4 in. (10.2 cm.); clenched fist provides handle for ivory bodkin, 5⅛ in. (13.0 cm.). *Sources:* Anonymous, 71.56; Harold H. Kynett, 41.632.8, 41.297.3, 41.297.4

implement. A somewhat more refined ivory piece [94], part of a collection of items believed to be the work of Fred Smith of *Ohio* fame, boasts a turned acorn finial.

The hand motif is evident on a pair of ivory bodkins. The shaft on the first piece [94] is merely a continuation of the hand, with its extended fingers. Completing this particular bodkin are decorative red bands encircling the shaft. The second specimen [94] incorporates the more familiar clenched fist design, separated from the shaft by a tiny collar of baleen.

An unusual fish motif appears on two very similar bodkins, probably the work of the same hand. The plainer of the two pieces defines the basic shape, with the shaft protruding from the fish's mouth. The more elaborate example [95] is of almost identical profile but features a more refined and detailed appearance. Deep crosshatching on the piece imparts a realistic fish-scale effect, in addition to the red and black ornamentation.

A woman's head and neck create the handle of a turned, heavily scribed ivory bodkin [95] in the collection. At 6³⁄₈ inches it is one of the larger examples in the Museum. The rather stiff demeanor of the face is reminiscent of early portrait photographs. An inlaid ring of baleen provides a visual accent as well as a physical transition between turned shaft and engraved head.

"Ball in cage" work, in which a free-rolling ball moves within a columned cage, testifies to the skill of some scrimshanders. One unknown artist managed to reduce this device [95] to a size under one inch in length and incorporate it in a bodkin that measures only 3¹⁄₄ inches overall. Atop the cage is a geometric design, the faceted cube, which serves as a knob handle.

Highly elaborate openwork handles characterize a number of ivory bodkins that could easily have been used as hairpins. One such piece [95] was obviously made from walrus ivory, as the crystalline core material is much in evidence. The outline of the

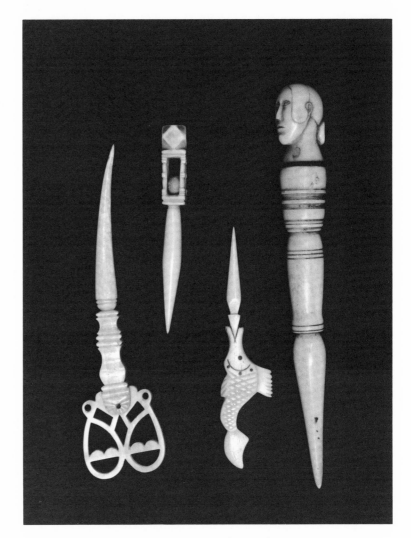

95. Unusual bodkin designs include, from left, heart-shaped openwork handle, 5¹⁄₄ in. (13.3 cm.); "ball in cage" work, 3¹⁄₄ in. (8.3 cm.); crosshatched "fish-scale" style, 3⁷⁄₈ in. (9.8 cm.); and carved female figure with baleen neck ring, 6³⁄₈ in. (16.2 cm.). *Sources:* Harold H. Kynett, 41.631.19, 41.413.2; Charles E. White, 39.2093; Harold H. Kynett, 41.297.9

96. A sampling of ivory needleholders featuring, left to right, sentimental heart motif, 2¼ in. (5.7 cm.); pedestal shape with baleen inlay, 3⁵⁄₁₆ in. (8.4 cm.); simple pierced square, 2 in. (5.1 cm.); and elaborate tortoiseshell and mother-of-pearl overlay, 3⅜ in. (8.6 cm.). *Sources:* Charles E. White, 39.2069; Museum purchase, 57.91; Harold H. Kynett, 41.631.10; Charles E. White, 39.2006

attached handle is clearly heart-shaped, adding a sentimental touch to the item.

Another sewing aid produced by the scrimshander was the needle holder. Normally made of whalebone or ivory, these objects were often carved or decorated with hearts and other sentimental motifs. Capable of holding one or more needles, these small accessories were designed to be sewn or pinned on a woman's bodice.

Four needle holders [96] from the Seaport's collection serve to illustrate the variety of design possible. All are of ivory, and two of them incorporate inlays and overlays of baleen, tortoiseshell, and mother-of-pearl.

While sewing thimbles were fabricated from bone and ivory, what is rarer is an ivory thimble case. One sailor combined craftsmanship with artistic talent to produce a finely turned

acorn-shaped thimble case [97]. The lid, which is threaded and screws onto the case, is itself turned, and decorated with red scroll leaf designs.

More elaborate scrimshaw items were also fabricated for the many sewing tasks faced by women in the nineteenth century. Special stands designed to hold spools of thread were contructed by shipboard craftsmen using familiar materials like bone, ivory, baleen, and wood. One all-ivory piece [98] is designed to hold four spools of thread at one time. Metal rods capped with turned finials slip through the spool holes, holding the spools in place. A tiny drawer in the two-inch-square base holds needles and other small items.

A larger spool holder [99] is designed to accommodate eighteen spools on two circular hardwood tiers. In this case the spool rods are whalebone, and the tiers are inlaid with ivory and mother-of-pearl, forming diamonds, circles, and an intricate sunburst pattern about the central wooden shaft. A trio of turned, scribed ivory legs supports the piece, which is topped by a red fabric pincushion. Museum records suggest that the 5¼-inch-diameter item was made sometime after the Civil War.

97. Acorn-shaped ivory thimble case boasts screw-on lid, 1⅝ in. (4.2 cm.). *Source:* Charles E. White, 39.2018

Rotating tiers distinguish a very elaborate spool holder [100] in the collection. Two round wood tiers have a total capacity of eleven spools, held in place by thin ivory rods. Each tier is supported by a turned ivory shaft at the center and similar, but smaller, columns at the edges. The 6½-inch-square base is characterized by a sawed fretwork border of wood and two storage drawers. Eight turned ivory posts with acorn finial

99 (below, left). Multi-tiered spool holder incorporates ivory and shell inlay and eighteen whalebone rods, 6¼ in. (15.9 cm.). *Source:* Mrs. H. B. Bradbury, 68.63

100 (below, right). Elaborate scrimshaw spool holder features rotating tiers and turned ivory supports with red scribings, 8½ in. (21.6 cm.). *Source:* Charles E. White, 39.1986

98 (above). Ivory spool holder includes drawer for needles and other sewing materials, 3¼ in. (8.3 cm.). *Source:* Anonymous, 70.314

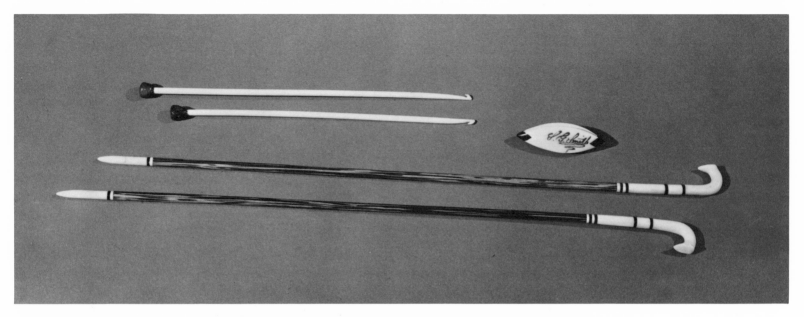

101. Specialized sewing items made for Sallie Smith by her husband Fred include whalebone crochet needles with red wax tips, 9⅝ in. (24.5 cm.) and 8¾ in. (22.2 cm.); ivory tatting shuttle marked "S. G. Smith," 2½ in. (6.4 cm.); and wood, ivory, and baleen knitting needles, 17⅝ in. (44.8 cm.). *Source:* Harold H. Kynett, 41.631.1ab, 41.632.17, 41.441, 41.442

decoration support this bottom tier, which in turn sits on four turned ivory legs. The turned central shaft and support posts are ornamented with red scribings. Tortoiseshell inlay visually accents the sides of the lowest tier, including the drawer faces, and is found on the upper levels as well. Ivory drawer knobs and facings add contrast to this ambitious piece. Topping this impressive effort is the familiar pincushion.

Other domestic implements like knitting needles were fair game for the scrimshander. Fred Smith apparently kept his wife Sallie well supplied with these utensils on one or more of their whaling voyages. Several pairs of these needles survive in the Museum today, including one fourteen-inch -long set fashioned

of whalebone with composite handles of wood, ivory, and baleen.

This same scrimshander adopted a different approach on another pair of needles [101], believed to have been made together with the previous set. Using wood reported to be from Chile's Juan Fernandez Islands, visited in 1883 while commanding the bark *John P. West*,[10] Smith constructed a pair of long knitting needles. Both the tapering tips and curved, umbrella-like handles were fashioned from ivory supplemented with baleen.

Another product of the 1875-1878 voyage of the *Ohio* was a pair of crochet needles [101]. Not surprisingly, these too were made by Fred Smith during some of the long months that passed between whale kills. Sallie noted in her journal that "Fred has made me some nice Crochet needles today and he has been learning how to use them."[11] These whalebone needles average nine inches and are capped by knobs of red sealing wax.

Sallie complained continually about the boredom she experienced aboard the *Ohio*. Her assumption of some navigational duties did little to fill the long hours. Even when whales were taken and the crew quite busy she could do nothing but watch. Little wonder, then, that Fred put so much effort into creating helpful items for his wife.

On 20 March 1878 Sallie noted that "Fred has made me a Tatting Shuttle and I have commenced to make Tattin."[12] This small ivory shuttle [101] is decorated in sepia ink with a five-pointed star on one side and the name "S. G. Smith" on the reverse. Sallie used the piece occasionally during the remaining seven months of the *Ohio*'s cruise.

The *ne plus ultra* of scrimshaw sewing equipment, and perhaps of scrimshaw as a whole, is the swift. For number of pieces required, complexity of operation, and beauty of design it is difficult to top these intricate and ingenious wool winders. Briefly, the swift consists of a folding basket-like reel that swivels on a vertical shaft. Swifts can be freestanding with their own legs, attached to the lids of fancy storage or sewing boxes, or designed to clamp onto the edge of a table or arm of a chair. A skein of yarn is placed over the expandable reel that holds it in place. One person can then proceed to wind the yarn neatly into a ball. As the yarn is taken up the reel swivels round and round. Most swifts incorporate a cup finial at the top of the shaft that is

102. Finely detailed ivory fist is an integral part of this scrimshaw swift, 12½ in. (31.8 cm.).
Source: Mrs. Raynham Townshend, 47.1449

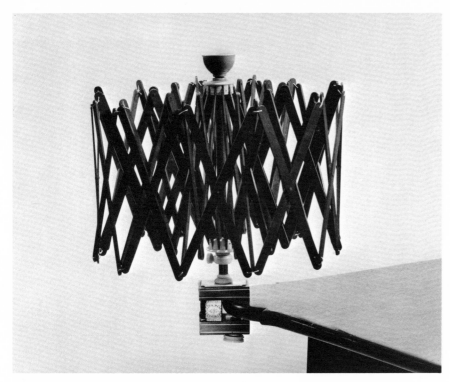

103. Striking ebony swift features ivory and mother-of-pearl ornamentation, 13½ in. (34.3 cm.). *Source:* Mrs. Henry H. Palmer, 63.268

designed to hold the ball of yarn should an interruption occur. Once the winding is completed the umbrella-like reel mechanism folds up, allowing the swift to be stored in a small box.

Many swifts require over one hundred pieces, including ribs, shaft sections, sliding sleeve, and locking screw, etc. Ribs are often fastened together with wire, rivets, and decorative ribbons. Whalebone, ivory, baleen, and wood are the usual raw materials employed in swifts, described by one author as "stunts of mechanical craftsmanship."[13] In view of the complexity of the swift it probably required an experienced scrimshander to execute such a work.

Swifts vary in size and intricacy of design and decoration.

One example [see color plate opp. p. 96] consists of a heavily turned bone and ivory shaft with a reel alone composed of 144 separate rib sections, fastened with rivets and variously colored ribbons. A thumbscrew clamp arrangement allows this swift to be attached to the edge of a table. What is particularly striking about this piece is the elaborate inlay of abalone at the base, the colored scribings on the shaft, and the green leaf decoration on the cup finial. No beginner's luck here, but rather the result of many months of patient labor by a master of this art.

The hand motif appears again, this time as the base of a whalebone and ivory winding swift [102]. This example uses the clenched fist as an integral part of the table clamp arrangement, which sits perpendicular to the shaft. The symbolism here is thought to suggest the idea of giving, though the argument has been made that it also demonstrates the proper manner for holding the swift. Complementing the ivory fist is a carved double cuff, perhaps of very light baleen or tortoiseshell, plus mother-of-pearl disks inlaid around the cup finial and sliding sleeve. Metal rivets and faded silk tassels secure the ribs together.

An example of inlaid wood construction is a swift [103] made of ebony. The use of white ivory in the cup finial, sliding sleeve, and locking screw provides a striking contrast to the black, tightly grained wood. Mother-of-pearl inlays around the clamp arrangement are engraved with floral designs and flanked with thin ivory inlays. This winder, which even incorporates a thin slice of elephant ivory in its ornamentation, is truly a masterpiece of scrimshaw design and execution.

Occasionally special storage boxes were constructed to hold the folded swift when not in use. Such is the case with a particularly large specimen [104] that measures fully two feet in height. The ribs alone equal the total height of the ebony swift. This heavy-duty winder is equipped with turned and

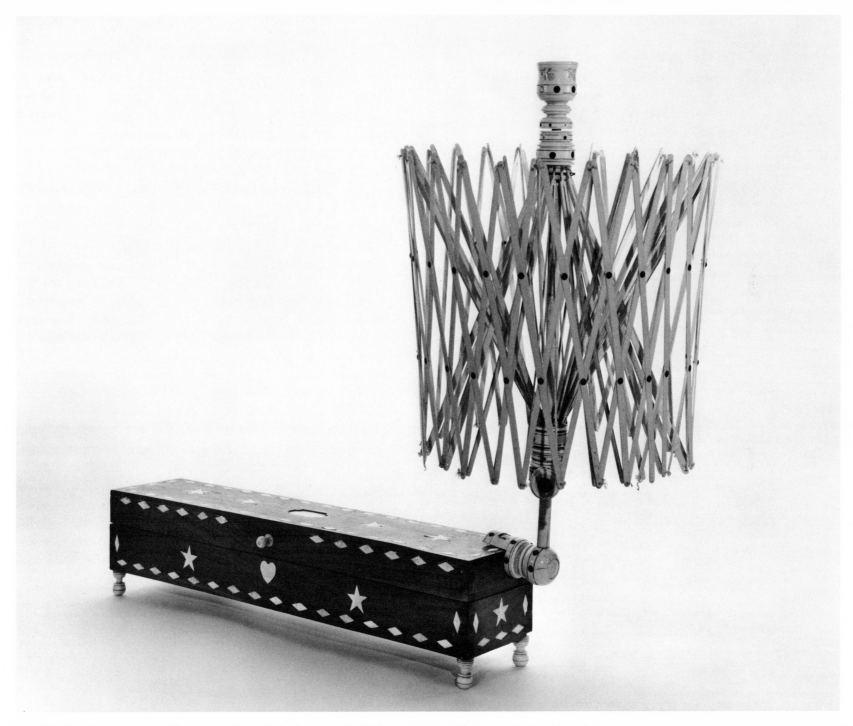

104. Viselike clamp secures this large swift, 24½ in. (62.2 cm.). Mahogany storage box can also double as base, 25⅛ x 5¹/₁₆ in. (63.8 x 12.8 cm.). *Source:* Mrs. Geneva Holmes Huston, 64.1134, 64.1135

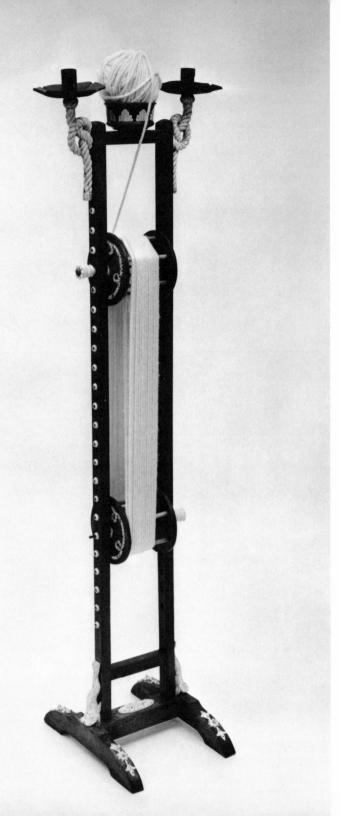

heavily inlaid ivory finial, sliding sleeve, and base clamp sections. These same pieces are further decorated with turned scribings filled with red sealing wax, while the cup finial bears exquisite floral engraving. Several silver coins, including one dated 1830, are inset in ivory portions of the swift. The viselike clamp attaches handily to the side of the storage box.

The twenty-five-inch-long box [104] itself is a worthy example of the scrimshander's art. Besides its storage function, the mahogany carrier serves as a floor base for the swift. A semicircular slot in one side allows the swift to clamp as if to the edge of a table. Some ninety-two separate ivory inlays, including stars, diamonds, and a heart, adorn this box, which also has four turned ivory legs and a round ivory handle. A blank ivory nameplate is centered on the lid. The swift and box are believed to have a New Bedford connection, though little else is known of the pair.

An unusual variation of this sewing aid is the "squirrel cage swift," so called because of the two horizontally mounted cylindrical winding wheels that resemble those revolving animal cages. Yarn is held between two small, adjustable reels rather than by the single, larger reel of a standard swift. The Museum's one example [105] of this item stands over forty-three inches in height. The wooden framework is highlighted with inlaid and applied whalebone and ivory decoration. A pair of stylized ivory dolphin brackets accompany ivory inlays on the feet. Most astounding of all is the elaborately carved whalebone knotwork that supports a pair of candleholders at the top of the piece. A composite cup of wood and ivory rests atop the uppermost

105. Wood, whalebone, and ivory "squirrel cage" swift incorporates two adjustable reels for holding skein of yarn, 43⅜ in. (110.2 cm.). *Source:* Harold H. Kynett, 41.514

crosspiece. Unfortunately, no history is available to answer the questions of who crafted the winder and when.

The many small sewing accessories created by the shipboard scrimshander often required secure storage containers to prevent their getting lost, either on shipboard or at home. By the same token the many balls of yarn, scraps of cloth, and other materials used in sewing also required a relatively compact means of stowage. The variously named work box, sewing box, or, in the case of sailors, ditty box served such an organizational purpose. That scrimshanders produced many of these items is not surprising. What is surprising is the range of materials and styles employed in their construction.

Baleen, with its flexible qualities, lent itself readily to use in these utility boxes. One of the several examples in the Museum [106] displays the characteristic round shape and is elaborately,

107. Panbone from the sperm whale provided the material for the rugged oval ditty box at left, 7^{15}/$_{16}$ x 10^{1}/$_{4}$ in. (20.2 x 26.0 cm.). Versatile panbone also supplied a scrimshander with the means to produce this delicate oval latticework sewing basket, 6^{1}/$_{2}$ x 9^{1}/$_{2}$ in. (16.5 x 24.1 cm.). *Source:* Harold H. Kynett, 52.44; Mrs. Charles H. Martin, 47.1747

106. Elaborate seam construction covers a portion of the incised decoration on this baleen ditty box. Note the commercial building with hanging shop sign at lower left, diam. 6^{7}/$_{8}$ in. (17.5 cm.). *Source:* Mrs. Alexander O. Vietor, 81.64.2

and skillfully, engraved with a selection of themes. A variety of structures, including a mansion, commercial building, and church, occupy a portion of the side. The balance of the box is devoted to a trio of square-rigged vessels. This handsome piece features a lid with sides heavily etched, this time with geometric, architectural, and floral embellishments. The intricate side seam incorporates heart-shaped cutouts in its construction. Like most other baleen boxes the lid top and base are made of wood. A variety of copper, brass, and iron brads fasten the piece together.

Another familiar cetacean by-product, panbone from the sperm whale, was adapted for use in boxes. Like baleen, it could be planed thin, engraved, and finally steamed and bent into shape. One whaleman did just this and produced an exquisite oval box [107] now in the Museum. A detailed repeat floral pattern, probably pin-pricked using a printed illustration, and retaining traces of original yellow inking, occupies nearly one full side of the 10¼-inch-long box. The reverse is committed to depictions of a merchant bark and a bark-rigged sidewheel warship in harbor. The scrimshander's own occupation is memorialized on the panbone lid in the form of an engraved scene featuring two whaleboats attacking a large sperm whale. Inlaid baleen encircles the top of the lid, while the lid sides feature a vinework motif. The quality of artistic effort in no way hides the fact that this is a very rugged piece of craftsmanship.

"I have sewed some and helped Fred he is making a box of bone."[14] Thus did Sallie Smith record the origin of a spectacular oval bone ditty box [108] while aboard the bark *Ohio* in December 1877. Fred and Sallie's handiwork is a prime example of top-notch scrimshaw. Like the previous box this piece is constructed of panbone and fancily seamed on one side. But what separates this box from the other is the lid. Using several types of wood as well as ivory, baleen, and horn, the Smiths have reproduced a compass rose pattern with rare skill. At the very center of the design is a small gold charm in the shape of a framed vine pattern. A combination of iron and copper fastenings secures the sides and ends of this superb, documented piece which, for comparison, measures 8⅝ inches in length.

Mother-of-pearl and other shellwork are usually relegated to a minor or supporting role in most scrimshaw items, but one small box [see color plate opp. p. 97] in the Seaport collection makes the most of this iridescent material. Captain John R. Stivers, in 1860 master of the New Bedford whaleship *Cicero*, chose colorful abalone to sheath a small hinged box he had built. Besides this shell the box also incorporates inlays of ivory, baleen, and possibly ebony in floral designs. The interior is

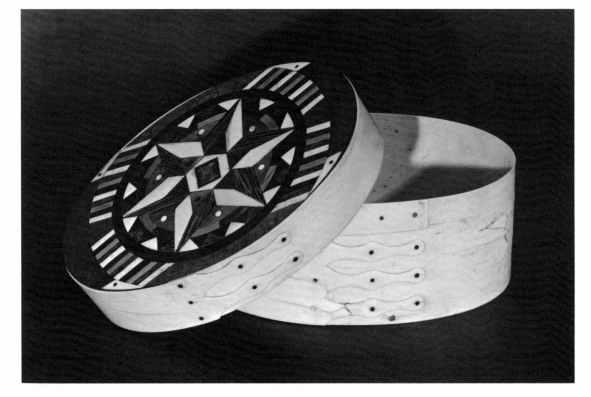

108. Oval whalebone ditty box made by Fred and Sallie Smith is distinguished by inlaid compass rose pattern on lid, 6½ x 8⅝ in. (16.5 x 21.9 cm.). *Source:* Harold H. Kynett, 41.399

109. Painstakingly inlaid rosettes and pinwheels of ivory, wood, and baleen ornament this wood and ivory work box, 9¼ x 13 in. (23.5 x 33.0 cm.). *Source:* Museum purchase, 65.791

Small baskets were also utilized for storing yarn and other sewing materials. Representative of several similar pieces in the Seaport is an oval whalebone latticework basket [107]. Constructed on a wooden base, this piece uses narrow whalebone strips to form the sides, to which is attached a thin whalebone handle. Brass pins fasten the ribs of this delicate yet useful article of scrimshaw.

Household Items

A wide range of articles for general household, or even shipboard, use were produced aboard whalers and other merchant vessels in the last century. A brief sampling of some domestic articles in the Museum's scrimshaw collection, some common, others probably unique, will suggest the variety of such items created at the hands of the scrimshander.

An old wooden pipe box [110], reportedly from Maine, presents indisputable evidence of the whaleman's pastime. The 21⅛-inch-tall piece is inlaid with ivory hearts, diamonds, and stars. A sperm whale and the date 1794, both inlaid in ivory, and five carved rosettes complete the box's decoration. This is a very early piece indeed.

Walrus ivory provided the raw material for a handsome pair of turned candlesticks [111] owned and possibly made by Captain Edwin W. White of New London, Connecticut. Red wax fills deep grooves on the shafts while a square base of wood and ivory slabs provides stability for the pair. Turned ivory acorn finials mark each corner, and decorative mother-of-pearl disks complete these candlesticks.

By the early nineteenth century oil lamps were fast replacing candles as a source of illumination. In response to the need to raise the wick of an oil lamp there developed the needle-like

fitted with green velvet, and a mirror sits under the lid. Four whale ivory feet support the box, which could have been used for storing sewing gear, jewelry, or similar items. The box remained in the captain's family until 1940.

A skillful mixing of inlaid whale ivory, baleen, and various woods sets one particular wooden work box [109] apart. The scrimshander has painstakingly created a variety of geometric patterns, including rosettes, two and four petal pinwheels, stars, quarter rounds, and others. Sperm whales, the source of much of the inlay material, are also in evidence on the side panels. The lid of this hinged box has an unusual ivory lifting ring centered on a large pinwheel design. Unfortunately, the scrimshander included almost everything but his own identity, now lost to us.

110 (far left). Date of 1794 makes this ivory inlaid pipe box one of the oldest pieces in the scrimshaw collection, 21⅛ in. (53.7 cm.). *Source:* Harold H. Kynett, 41.280

111 (left). Pair of turned walrus ivory candlesticks owned by Captain Edwin W. White of New London, Connecticut, 8½ in. (21.6 cm.). *Source:* Charles E. White, 39.1932, 39.1933

112 (below). Whale ivory wick-picks: left, a turned and scribed example with wax decoration, 3⅜ in. (8.6 cm.); right, a bell-shaped base for stability, 3⅝ in. (9.2 cm.). *Sources:* Harold H. Kynett, 41.422; Museum purchase, 52.49

wick-pick. Handles of wood, bone, ivory, and other materials were often attached to these picks, and naturally enough scrimshanders added their own refinements. Several scrimshaw wick-picks in the Museum collection testify to this new shipboard interest. One ivory piece [112] is heavily turned and decorated with red and blue wax. Besides a turned finial handle the wick-pick also has a wide turned ivory base providing stability, even on shipboard. An even more stable design is found in another ivory wick-pick [112], turned in the shape of a bell. The long grip serves as a handle for the pick, which is recessed in the base when not in use.

An unknown scrimshander devised a means of turning a simple pocket watch into a distinctive timepiece for home use. Using whalebone, baleen, and whale ivory, both teeth and

113. Functional beauty: scrimshaw clock stand incorporates wood, whalebone, and whale ivory, 13½ in. (34.3 cm.).
Source: Museum purchase, 52.41

slices, he constructed a marvelous clock stand [113]. A multi-tiered wooden base supported by four ivory legs provides the foundation. Upon this is centered a quartet of ivory slabs in terrace fashion, the top slab inlaid with baleen. Rising vertically is a façade composed of a splendid matched pair of whale teeth engraved with full-rigged British ships. Between the teeth is a square slab of panbone pierced by a viewing port for the watch dial and topped by a pair of turned finials and a center pedestal designed to hold the watch fob. A wooden pocket on the back of this slab cradles the timepiece. This masterpiece of form and function stands slightly over 7½ inches in height.

Another type of household accessory was the inkstand, and here too a shipbound artist tried his hand. The Museum's example [114] consists of a generally rectangularly shaped

wooden base sitting on six S-curve ivory legs. An ivory bail handle is attached to each of the two narrow ends of the base. Inlays of ivory and possibly ebony decorate the top of the stand, the ivory end pieces being engraved with American shields. Two raised oval ivory rings, designed to hold ink bottle and sander, are placed at the center, while carved ivory brackets in the shape of shields serve as pen cradles. The grain of the ivory suggests that a walrus tusk, not a whale tooth, was the source of this material.

The ornate inkstand was fine for use at a large desk but in the cramped cabins of many ships space was at a premium. Small portable lap desks, also useful when traveling away from home, were the answer to this problem. Among the Seaport's holdings is a superb example [115] constructed of ebony. A fold-out

114. Thin slices of a walrus tusk probably supplied the bottle rings atop this elaborately constructed inkstand, 10⅞ in. (27.6 cm.). *Source:* Harold C. Lyman, 40.95

115. Ebony lap desk features unusually fine ivory inlay and use of red wax in keyhole shield, 8⅝ x 14½ in. (21.9 x 36.8 cm.). *Source:* Harold H. Kynett, 41.374

writing surface and recessed slots for ink bottle, sander, paper, and pens would be found inside such a desk. Ivory inlays on the lid and side include the familiar pinwheel design along with stars, diamonds, and lovebirds. The shield-shaped ivory keyhole plate on the front is itself inlaid with red sealing wax, adding the only other touch of color found on the piece.

The quality of the workmanship and the richness of the materials suggest that this 14½ by 8⅝ inch desk was not made in a crowded fo'c'sle, but rather in the cabin of a whaleship officer experienced at this type of craft.

Brushes are used in any number of household functions, so it comes as no surprise that scrimshanders occasionally fabricated such items. For everyday dusting of furnishings at home or in a ship's cabin, a horsehair brush, for example, with a whalebone handle like one found in the collection, would be quite suitable.

A scrimshaw brush of a distinctly more personal nature is also part of the Seaport's holdings. This natural bristle toothbrush [116] with inlaid ivory handle, while unusual, suggests the potential range of articles that a gifted practitioner could produce. Ivory, baleen, and tortoiseshell decoration accent the fine ivory shaft of this well-used implement.

The humble clothespin was not neglected by whalemen in their leisure time activity. Sallie Smith mentioned in her *Ohio* journal that Fred had made three clothespins for her. Two months later, in September 1877, she noted that "Fred finished the last of three Dozen Clothes pins for me."[15] Among the several dozen whalebone clothespins in the Museum is one

116. Scrimshaw odds and ends: from top, unusual toothbrush sports inlaid handle, 7 in. (17.8 cm.); plain, functional whalebone clothespin, possibly by Fred Smith, 4 in. (10.2 cm.); and finely turned and scribed whalebone clothespin, 4 in. (10.2 cm.). *Sources:* Charles E. White, 39.1918; Harold H. Kynett, 41.631.3b; Charles E. White, 39.2031

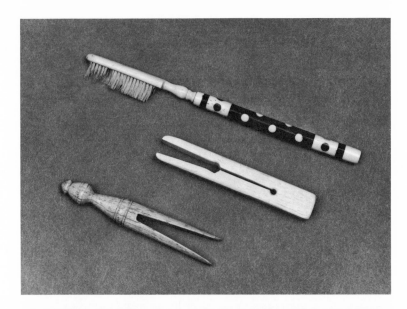

[116] of several believed to have been made by the captain aboard the *Ohio.* Fred's square, no-nonsense pin stands in marked contrast to one of the more stylized examples [116] in our collection.

Furniture and large household items are less likely candidates for construction by scrimshanders, especially in light of the amount of space, quantity of materials, and joiner skills required for such undertakings. In spite of these obstacles such items were indeed fabricated by certain scrimshanders. A 19⅛-inch-tall birdcage [117], for example, required a prodigious amount of whalebone and effort; but the maker must certainly have been impressed with the finished product.

Perhaps a ship's carpenter fashioned a wooden footstool [118] inlaid with strips of whalebone. A New Bedford origin is ascribed to this piece, with its bone stars, strips, and diamonds.

The search for the perfect coatrack ended with the creation of an item which can safely be termed unique. The rack [119] consists of a heavy, turned wooden shaft and shelf supported by four cannonball feet. Turned pieces of ivory at the top of the shaft provide hooks for hat or coat. What sets this article of furniture apart, however, are the four narwhal tusks, with turned ivory supports, mounted upright from the feet of the

117. This full-sized whalebone birdcage is a testament to the skill and patience of an unknown scrimshander, 19⅛ x 16¾ x 12⅜ in. (48.6 x 42.5 x 31.4 cm.). *Source:* Harold H. Kynett, 41.277

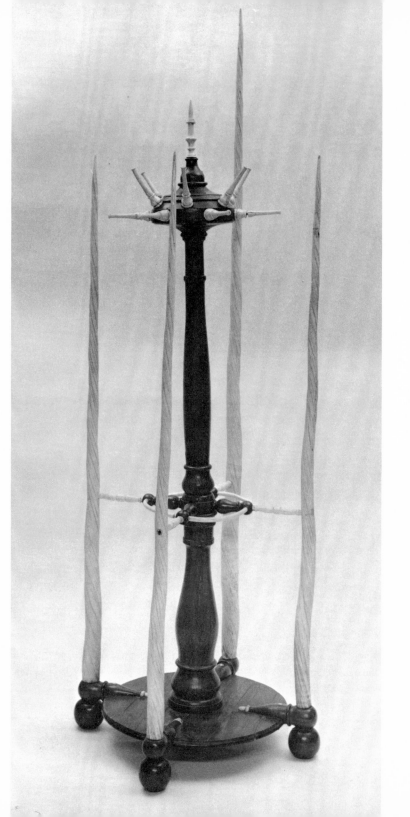

118 (above). Utility and style combine in this inlaid footstool, 7³/8 x 16 x 7⁷/8 in. (18.7 x 40.6 x 20.0 cm.). *Source:* Harold H. Kynett, 41.598

119 (right). This spectacular wood, walrus ivory, and narwhal tusk coatrack is almost certainly unique, 7 ft. 6¹/2 in. (229.8 cm.). *Source:* Dr. John G. Murray, 64.1227

120 (below). Scrimshaw games and toys: ebony and bone dominoes each measure 1¹¹/16 x ⁵/8 in. (4.3 x 1.6 cm.); ivory mortar and pestle each stand ³/4 in. (1.9 cm.) tall; and miniature whalebone rifle is 3⁵/8 in. (9.2 cm.) long. *Sources:* Richard H. and Willis S. Fuller, 65.767; Estate of Alice S. Bishop, 64.73; Charles E. White, 39.2101

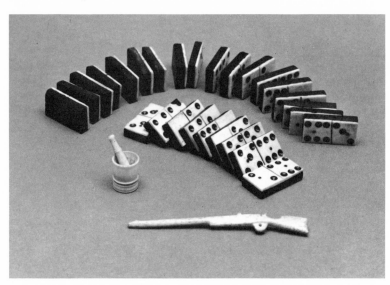

121. Unusual toy deckhouse is built completely of decorated sheets of panbone, 1¹³/₁₆ x 4¹/₁₆ x 3¹⁵/₁₆ in. (4.6 x 10.3 x 10.0 cm.). *Source:* Museum purchase, 82.1.1

rack. A narwhal tusk is rare enough, but to acquire four of these trophies, ranging from five to seven feet in length, is truly astounding. No fo'c'sle piece, this. It is almost too large to fit in a ship's cabin and was no doubt intended for use ashore. Fragments of written evidence in Museum records mention a whaling captain in reference to this piece, but whether he was the maker is not known. It is possible that a ship's carpenter or other skilled crewman made the piece with materials furnished by this master.

Toys and games, like jewelry, were not made as often as other articles; or if they were, then few have survived intact. Several sets of whalebone dominoes have been preserved by the Museum. Here was a game that could be played with equal ease at home and afloat. One particular set [120] consists of some twenty-seven playing pieces made of bone and ebony. Black ink or paint appears to have been used in marking the dots.

Miniature toys fashioned by scrimshanders are rarely found. Among the handful in the collection is a tiny ivory mortar and pestle [120]. Neither piece stands more than ¾ inch in height. A different type of miniature is a finely carved whalebone rifle [120] measuring only 3⅝ inches.

Quite possibly a unique item is the toy ship's deckhouse [121] created by an unknown craftsman. Constructed solely of thin panbone sheets, the 4¹/₁₆-inch-long house is pierced with eight windows and four doorways. A center partition divides the structure into two separate cabins, while the phrase "Good

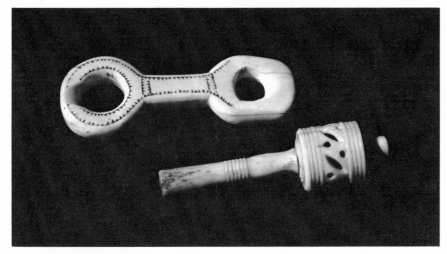

122. Infants' toys include, at top, a well-used ivory teething ring, 4⅜ in. (11.1 cm.); and a combination rattle and whistle, 3¾ in. (9.5 cm.). *Sources:* Anonymous, 70.104; Charles E. White, 39.2107

123. Coconut shell dippers were fashioned with a wide variety of handles. At top, wood handle incorporates slices of whale ivory and baleen for contrast, 17 in. (43.2 cm.); Captain Fred Smith is the probable creator of the ivory-handled example at center, 14½ in. (36.8 cm.); below, an unusual scrimshaw kitchen aid is this whalebone meat mallet, 9½ in. (24.1 cm.). *Sources:* Charles E. White, 39.1926; Harold H. Kynett, 41.403; Mrs. Alexander O. Vietor, 81.64.4

Luck" appears on the two end walls. Bold diamond patterns in several colors decorate the roof, floor, and walls of this unusual piece.

Among the diversions intended for infants is a well-worn ivory teething ring [122] replete with incised sawtooth decoration. A complete child's rattle [122] made of ivory and whalebone is also in the collection. In this instance, a small bell puts the "rattle" in the rattle, but what is more unusual is the fact that the hollow whalebone handle has been converted into a whistle. Recent tests indicate that both rattle and whistle functions are fully operational.

Kitchen Utensils

In the days before Cuisinarts, frozen dinners, and other conveniences, a woman spent a good deal of time preparing food for herself and family. A wide variety of utensils, some familiar to us, others long outmoded, were necessary fixtures in the nineteenth-century kitchen. To this need many scrimshanders responded, producing an astonishing array of culinary aids.

Sallie Smith noted in her *Ohio* journal that "Fred finished the second dipper for me today."[16] Though she did not elaborate, this piece is possibly the one dipper [123] in our collection credited to Captain Smith. Like most scrimshaw dippers, this example has a bowl made from a hollowed coconut shell. An ivory handle composed of six segments with alternating wood spacers is attached to the bowl by copper fastenings. The ivory section joined to the bowl is carved in the shape of a heart, while the opposite end of the handle carries a threaded ivory hanging ring. This 14½-inch-long dipper stands as another tribute to the scrimshaw talents of Fred Smith.

The unnamed creator of another coconut dipper [123] employed almost the reverse technique in fashioning his handle. Here a five-section mahogany grip incorporates whale ivory and baleen spacers. The ivory segment attached directly to the bowl shares the same heart shape as Fred Smith's handiwork. A somewhat larger piece than Smith's, this dipper measures seventeen inches.

Another apparent product of Fred Smith's shipboard labors is a simple scoop for use with flour, sugar, or other staples. A piece of uncut panbone, perhaps from a small whale or one of the many porpoises Smith caught during his voyages, provides the basis for this scoop, the wooden handle of which appears to have been appropriated from a paint brush.

A rather unusual item, but one helpful in the face of poor-quality meats, is the whalebone meat mallet [123] found in the Museum. Useful in dredging meat as well as taming some of the wilder cuts, this mallet includes one deeply crosshatched face for tenderizing and one smooth face for shaping meats.

Captain Stephen Morgan, a whaling master believed to have hailed from Ledyard, Connecticut, is credited with creating an unusual set of serving items sometime in the first half of the nineteenth century. Using hollowed coconut shells and whale ivory, Morgan produced a number of table bowls and related items [124]. A total of seven pieces in the collection, including a pair of creamers and sugar bowls, are attributed to Morgan, who signed or initialed several of these items. The hinged lid of one sugar bowl is marked "A D/1831" suggesting that the other half dozen pieces date to this period as well. Fine floral engraving is visible on several of these table accessories.

At nearly the same time that Morgan was producing cocount shell and ivory serving pieces, another whaleman was also busy preparing dining items. A matched set of four whalebone spoons [125], each averaging 4¾ inches, testifies to the labor of this anonymous craftsman. The spoons are marked "MARY,"

124. Coconut shell and ivory serving items made by Captain Stephen Morgan, c. 1831. Left to right, creamer, 4½ in. (11.4 cm.); engraved bowl, 4¾ in. (12.1 cm.); and sugar bowl, 5 in. (12.7 cm.). *Source:* Mrs. Annie M. Brown, 39.383, 39.386, 39.385

125. Set of whalebone spoons marked "ANNA," "MARY," "FANNY," and "JENNIE," dated 1827, 4¾ in. (12.1 cm.). *Source:* Mrs. Raynham Townshend, 47.1415, 47.1416, 47.1418, 47.1419

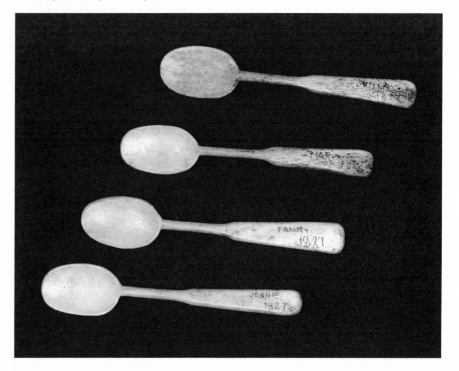

126. Whale ivory table set crafted by Fred Smith includes a pair of funnels, 3⅝ in. (9.2 cm.); and three napkin rings averaging 1½ in. (3.8 cm.) diam. An ivory pie crimper, 7⅛ in. (18.1 cm.), and butter knife, 6¼ in. (15.9 cm.), are both marked with Sallie Smith's initials. *Source:* Harold H. Kynett, 41.396.5-6, 41.396.1-3, 41.632.2, 41.632.6

"JENNIE," "ANNA," and "FANNY" respectively, and each bears the engraved date 1827. Perhaps these small spoons were made by the whaleman for his four daughters back home.

It is well established that Fred Smith responded to his wife's kitchen requirements with a variety of scrimshaw items. But by the same token that veteran whaleman did not overlook the desirability of certain dining accessories. A 6¼-inch-long ivory butter knife [126] probably graced the Smiths' dining table on one or more whaling voyages. Diamond-shaped mother-of-pearl inlay and Sallie's inked initials "s. G. s." adorn the handle.

In addition to this knife Captain Smith is believed to have produced a trio of napkin rings [126] patterned in checkerboard, spiral, and pinched waist designs respectively. Accompanying these is what at first glance appears to be an ivory egg cup, but which is more likely an open salt. Red wax highlights the delicately turned scribing on this piece. Two sperm whale teeth provided the basis for a pair of funnels [126], again work attributed to the *Ohio*'s master. Hollowed out and equipped with narrow ivory spouts at the tips, these funnels allowed the filling of small spice shakers and similar containers. One piece is decorated with red scribings and an engraved salt and pepper set.

A survey of scrimshaw kitchen utensils leads to the conclusion that, in the eyes of the shipbound scrimshander at least, pie baking was the supreme culinary art. In order to encourage such good work a veritable barrage of baking accessories poured ashore, destined for the hearths, if not the hearts, of wives and girl friends.

Rolling pins of all shapes and sizes returned home with their seagoing makers during the last century. Especially useful in the making of pies and pastry, these heavy rollers were often intended as presents. Even if not actually used in pie making, the rolling pin clearly suggested the homecoming sailor's keen

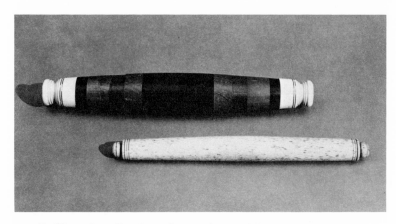

127. Rolling pins of various sizes and materials were produced on shipboard. The multi-sectioned example is possibly the work of Josiah Robinson, 15 in. (38.1 cm.); below, an unusual whalebone rolling pin, 13 3/16 in. (33.5 cm.). *Sources:* Harold H. Kynett, 41.291; Mrs. Alexander O. Vietor, 81.64.15

interest in sampling the tasty results of bakeday activities.

Most rolling pins combine wooden roller with ivory or whalebone handles. Among the dozen rolling pins in the collection is one that features ivory disks inlaid on the roller. This type of ornamentation appears to be the exception rather than the rule in the construction of these items.

Josiah Robinson (b. 1837) of Mattapoisett, Massachusetts, served aboard whalers in the second half of the nineteenth century. A collection of tools believed to have been made by him[17] suggests that he was a ship's carpenter or possibly a cooper. Among the kitchen items attributed to his hand is a fine rolling pin [127], probably for his wife, Lucy C. Robinson. Composed of nine sections featuring several different woods, among them lignum vitae, the fifteen-inch-long pin includes ivory handles, probably turned on Robinson's own small lathe, which, incidentally, is also part of the Seaport collection [135]. Red wax

decoration outlines some of the turning work while mother-of-pearl inlays adorn the handles.

An unusual rolling pin [127] is made entirely from a single large piece of whalebone. Almost all scrimshaw pins were made of dense hardwood to provide a smooth, nonstick surface. It is difficult to imagine how the grainy whalebone surface of this pin would fare in actual use, even with liberal and frequent applications of flour.

With the rolling of the pie dough completed, the next step was to cut the dough into the appropriate circle, strip, or whatever shape was required, and crimp the crusts together after filling the pie. A knife and fork might suffice for some cooks, but those desiring a more elaborate effect often looked to an implement variously known as a pie wheel, jagging wheel, or pie crimper. Basically this consisted of a fluted cutting and crimping wheel held within a handle. Sometimes the crimper was equipped with a short fork for poking steam vents in top crusts. A small whalebone example [128] illustrates the basic article.

Pie crimpers are among the most numerous types of surviving utilitarian items. Like the swift, the pie crimper allowed the whaleman to combine elements of artistry and engineering in a single piece. Perhaps Ashley was a bit carried away when he pronounced the pie crimper "the *chef d'oeuvre* on which [the scrimshander] was willing that his reputation should stand or fall,"[18] but there was obviously some widespread appeal in this kitchen tool. Different authors have waxed eloquent on the sublime qualities of nineteenth-century New England pies and the shipbound epicure's fixation with same; but none present truly convincing arguments to correlate this claim with the marked abundance of scrimshaw pie crimpers.

Certainly the pie crimper was a useful article appreciated by many women. Like a busk, the crimper could also be viewed as a

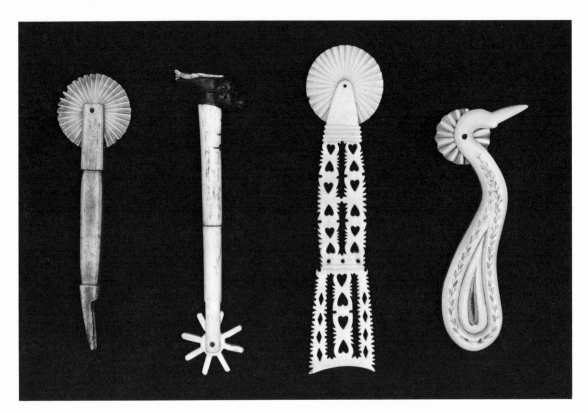

128. The scrimshander's *"chef-d'oeuvre,"* the pie crimper: left to right, the basic article, 6¾ in. (17.2 cm.); a piece dedicated to "wives and sweethearts," 7⅜ in. (18.7 cm.); lacy ivory handle distinguishes a large example, 8⅛ in. (20.7 cm.); and a "Big Bird" lookalike, 6⅛ in. (15.6 cm.). *Sources:* Estate of Alice S. Bishop, 64.74; Charles E. White, 39.1952; Museum purchase, 46.1481; Harold H. Kynett, 41.612

sentimental gesture or a keepsake from a loved one. This article could also serve as a challenge for a scrimshander bent on improving his carving skills. An additional factor is the possibility that an annual pie crimper exhibition and competition was held in New Bedford, with substantial prizes awarded for the best examples.[19]

Captain Fred Smith was not immune to the urge to produce a pie crimper for his wife, Sallie. Using whale ivory he fashioned just such a piece [126], inlaid it with thin slices of tortoiseshell, and added the now familiar "s. g. s." to the handle. A three-tined fork completes this 7⅛-inch-long utensil, which was probably used in the making of one of the Smiths' favorite shipboard dishes, "Whortleberrie pot pie."

Whereas Fred Smith was often happily accompanied on voyages by his spouse, another whaleman was obviously of a different mind. Engraved on the narrow whalebone shaft of a pie crimper [128] is the telling expression "Heres to our wives and/sweethearts/may they never meet."

A superb openwork handle distinguishes another crimper [128]. Eight pairs of hearts plus diamonds and a fretwork border lend a lacy quality to this ivory utensil. The handle consists of a single-layer end piece that is sandwiched between and fastened to an inner section composed of two thicknesses of ivory. The carved fork, an integral part of many crimpers, is not included on this example.

Sometimes pie crimpers were carved in the shape of animals.

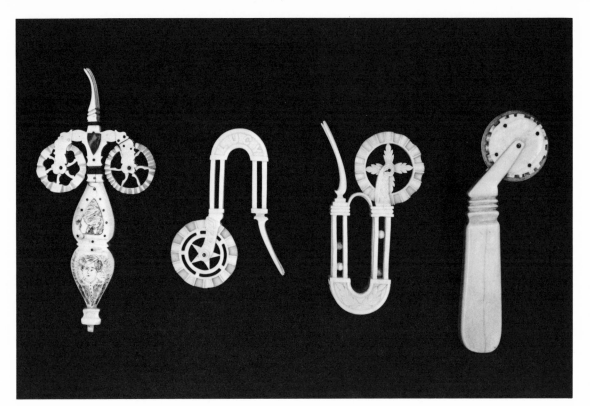

129. More pie crimpers: from left, an elaborate double wheel example featuring boy's portrait and mother-of-pearl inlay, 7¼ in. (18.4 cm.); piece marked "LUCY" is thought to be by whaleman Josiah Robinson, 4⅜ in. (11.1 cm.); U-shaped crimper incorporates "ball in cage" work, 5¼ in. (13.4 cm.); and heavy cutter wheel spells "GOOD PIE WELL MADE," 6¾ in. (17.2 cm.). *Sources:* Museum purchase, 46.1475; Harold H. Kynett, 41.297.1; Museum purchase, 46.1477; Mrs. Charles H. Martin, 47.1605

For example, a graceful, long-necked bird forms the framework of an ivory crimper [128] in the Seaport collection. Looking for all the world like the "Big Bird" character from "Sesame Street," this scrimshaw carving includes a three-tined fork in place of the bird's beak. Meanwhile the eyes of this *avis raris* are in fact the ends of the metal axle pin on which the wheel rotates. Finely engraved vinework ornaments the flanks of this ingenious creation.

Occasionally a scrimshander felt the need to include more than one wheel on a pie crimper. Of the multiple wheel crimpers in the Museum, one example [129] in particular seems to illustrate the fact that in the fashioning of these ostensibly utilitarian items "decoration frequently triumphs over practical-

ity."[20] Two differently carved wheels flank a center ivory shaft carved in the shape of inverted hearts. Engraved portraits of a boy on one side and a girl on the other are complemented by heart-shaped mother-of-pearl inlays. Tortoiseshell is used in both the construction and decoration of the shaft, which in turn is topped by a three-tined fork. It appears that the crimper once included a ring or some other type of hanging fixture at the base of the handle, though only a damaged bracket remains.

A pair of U-shaped ivory pie crimpers illustrates the extraordinary artistry and craftsmanship which could be bestowed upon such a piece by a talented scrimshander. The simpler of the pair [129] incorporates two rectangular chambers formed by parallel columns. Intricate floral relief carving accents the piece,

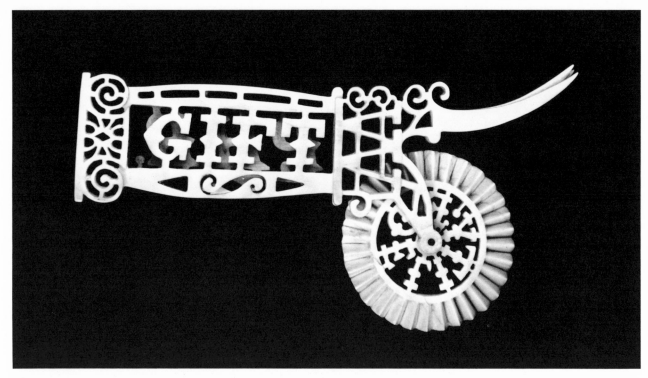

130. Superb example of the scrimshander's art is this whale ivory pie crimper, dated "July 15 1857." Wheel spokes spell "FIDELITY," 6⅝ in. (16.8 cm.). *Source:* Harold H. Kynett, 41.413.3

which bears the name "LUCY." This crimper is believed to have been made by Josiah Robinson for his wife Lucy sometime after the Civil War.

The second example [129] shares the same design but with more elaboration in places. The maker of this pie crimper added two more columned chambers and enclosed free-rolling ivory balls: another example of "ball in cage" work. Each tiny ball, incidentally, is scribed and decorated with red wax. Though Lucy's name is nowhere to be found on this piece, the very similar floral carving suggests the possibility that Robinson might be responsible for this crimper as well.

One of the more unusual pie crimpers [129] in the Museum

does not have the characteristic fluted wheel, but rather a straight edge like a pizza cutter. What makes this piece unusual, however, is the recessed edge of the cutting disk on which is carved reverse lettering in high relief. When used to cut dough, the crimper, with each full turn of the wheel, boldly prints along the edge the message "GOOD PIE WELL MADE." It pays to advertise.

Perhaps the masterpiece among the Museum's crimpers is an elaborate specimen [130] that includes a bit of built-in documentation. The openwork ivory handle bears the initials "P. H. R." on one side and the word "GIFT" on the opposite face. The bold initial "W" is an integral part of the construction and appears on both sides. The edge of the four-tined fork reads "JULY, 15" and the base of the handle completes the date with an engraved "1857." Countless hours must have been spent in achieving the intricate swirls and curlicues incorporated into the handle design. A final, very personal touch is added by the spokes of the wheel, which are in fact letters spelling out "FIDELITY." Although it is uncertain whether "P. H. R." is the scrimshander or the recipient, there is no mistaking the heart-felt sentiment that prompted the execution of this superb example of the scrimshander's art.

Tools and Other Gear

Whalebone's strength and durability, expecially when fresh, made it a natural candidate for use in rugged utilitarian pieces. Tools, and even portions of rigging, were fabricated from this abundant by-product of the whaling industry.

Some whaleships were known to use blocks and other fittings which were constructed at least in part of whalebone.[21] Several examples of this type of work appear in the collection, among them a large bronze-fastened block [131] measuring 6¼ inches in length. A single lignum vitae sheave, leather-bound rope strapping, and an iron hook complete this hefty piece, which approaches sixteen inches in overall length.

Differences in size and material distinguish another block in the Museum. A double sheave ivory block [131], one of a pair, features ivory, not wood sheaves, as well as copper fastenings. Though strong enough for some uses, this 4½-inch-long piece appears to have been displayed rather than employed in any shipboard function.

Heart-shaped thimbles for use in rigging, mooring lines, or wherever an open eye was required, were also fashioned from the bone of the sperm whale. One fine example [131] of this type of fitting measures 4⅛ inches.

Whaling voyages to arctic areas often saw some sealing activity as well. Sealing then, as now, involved the clubbing of the animals. On one such combined cruise to the Canadian arctic James Martin, a crewman aboard the New Bedford bark *Morning Star*, produced a club made from a walrus tusk. The 16½-inch-long bludgeon is inscribed "SEAL AND WALRUS PERSUADER" and "SHIP MORNING STAR/from NEW BEDFORD/to HUDSON BAY/Sept 30 1864." A harbor scene with walruses bears the identification "REPULSE BAY" and "BEADS HARBOUR." Martin made the club early in the vessel's seventeen-month cruise in northern waters. Commanded by Charles

131. Workaday scrimshaw items include blocks and other gear. Large single sheave whalebone block with hook measures 15⅞ in. (40.3 cm.); small ivory block has copper fastenings, 4½ in. (11.5 cm.); whalebone thimble combines form and function, 4⅛ in. (10.5 cm.). *Sources:* Mrs. Raynham Townshend, 47.1330; Museum purchase, 81.12.1; Mrs. Alexander O. Vietor, 81.64.12

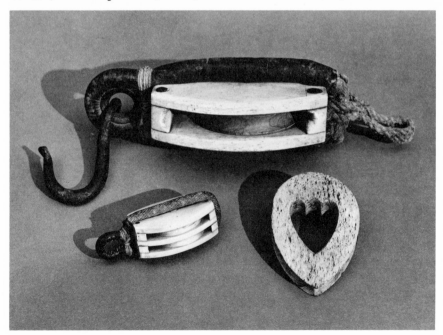

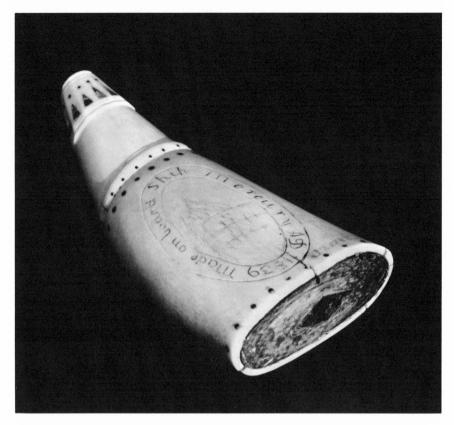

132. Small whale tooth powder horn was made aboard ship *Mercury* in 1839, 5½ in. (14.0 cm.). *Source:* Charles E. White, 39.1782

E. Allen, the 238-ton bark returned home in October 1865 with over 1100 barrels of whale oil. The sealskin tally was not noted in the whaling records.

An unusual shipboard accouterment found in the collection is a small powder horn [132] made from a sperm whale tooth. The tip of the hollowed-out tooth was removed and a plug, now missing, inserted in its place. The base was sealed off with a baleen plug and fastened with tiny brads. Thirteen triangular abalone inlays decorate the tip, while the side is engraved with the legend "Made on board Ship Mercury A D 1839." That year

both Stonington, Connecticut, and New Bedford claimed whaleships named *Mercury,* and it is impossible to determine to which vessel the powder horn refers. The complexity of the Roman pantheon managed to confuse this scrimshander, who engraved a likeness of Diana the huntress, not the messenger Mercury, on the reverse of the piece.

To assist in the splicing of lines, conical implements known as fids were used. The pointed end of the spike-shaped tool separated the rope strands so that another line might be spliced in.

133. Splicing work either afloat or ashore required the use of fids. These whalebone examples illustrating various styles of decoration measure, left to right, 12⅛ in. (30.8 cm.), 18¼ in. (46.3 cm.), and 14 in. (35.5 cm.). *Sources:* Dr. Charles K. Stillman, 36.49; Harold H. Kynett, 41.334; Mrs. Charles H. Martin, 47.1638

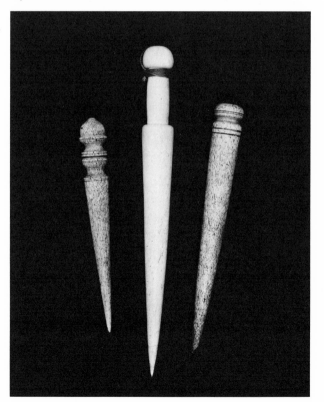

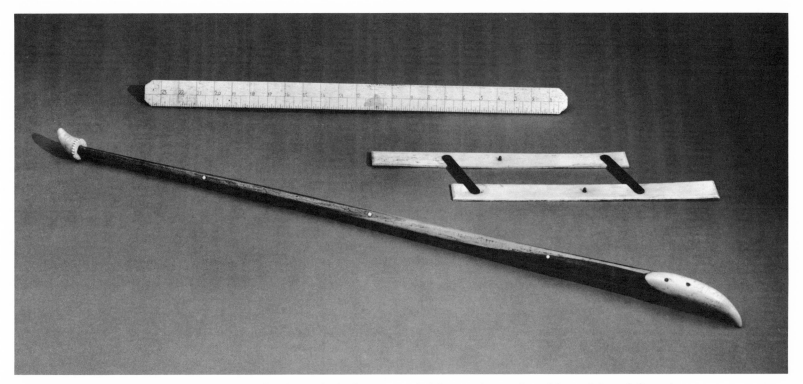

134. Scrimshaw straightedge devices in the collection include, from top, whalebone ruler numbered from right to left, 24 in. (61.0 cm.); brass-hinged whalebone parallel ruler for plotting courses, 13¾ in. (34.9 cm.); gauge stick made by George Townsend aboard whaler *Magnolia,* 36 in. (91.5 cm.). *Sources:* Dr. Charles K. Stillman, 36.109; Harold H. Kynett, 41.292; Mrs. Raynham Townshend, 47.1334

In addition to wood, whalebone was often used in the construction of these tools. Similar in shape to some bodkins, fids ranged in length from about 6 to over 18 inches. While many examples were crudely shaped, others exhibited a fair amount of craftsmanship. A selection of three whalebone fids [133] of from 12 to 18¼ inches illustrates some of the potential embellishments possible on these workaday items.

Certain types of measurements were required by shipboard coopers and carpenters. For example, to determine the amount of liquid in a cask a gauge stick was often used, much like the oil dipstick in an automobile engine. One George Townsend of the ship *Magnolia* produced such a gauge [134] using a variety of light and dark woods and pieces of whale ivory. Inlaid ivory dots are fixed at nine-inch intervals along the side of this yard-long rod, a practice similar to that used on early measuring sticks.[22]

What best distinguishes this canelike item from a walking stick or yardstick is the engraved legend found on the whale tooth handle: "GEORGE TOWNSEND/GAUGER/Ship MAGNOLIA/NEW BEDFORD/1857." The *Magnolia* was whaling in the North Pacific in 1857. Commanded by Captain G. L. Cox, the 396-ton ship returned home the following year with a large quantity of baleen and whale oil, but only a tiny amount of the higher quality sperm whale oil.

Linear measurements required different equipment, the most common being straightedge measuring sticks graduated in inches. Panbone, that thin whalebone from the sperm whale's jaw used in ditty boxes and other items, was a natural choice of many scrimshanders carving these tools. It could be cut in lengths of a yard or more and planed smooth, a necessity for some of these measuring devices. One of these scrimshaw rulers [134] in the Museum is a two-footer, graduated to ⅛ inch increments. Not surprisingly, that prolific scrimshander Fred Smith probably produced a whalebone ruler as well, this one divided into ¼ inch segments on one edge and approximately ⅙ inch sections on the opposite edge. Perhaps the piece was intended as a spacing guide on unruled writing paper.

A different type of rule attributed to Captain Smith was the whalebone parallel ruler [134] designed for use with navigational charts. Like its wood or metal counterparts, this bone plotting tool uses brass hinges to line up accurately the courses or bearings to be plotted. Each ruler measures 13¾ inches in length.

Josiah Robinson, Jr., the Mattapoisett whaleman, served aboard the bark *Cape Horn Pigeon* from 1869 to 1872 and possibly sailed on other vessels as well. The high quality of some of his scrimshaw work has been attributed in part to the fact that he apparently had a small lathe [135] at his disposal. Made of whalebone and metal on a wooden carriage, this 28¾-inch-long machine is believed to date from about 1867. From this lathe are said to have come such pieces as the rolling pin [127] described earlier in this chapter.

A selection of other, more rugged tools is also credited to the hand of this scrimshander. Among the pieces is a large whalebone mallet [136]. Perhaps intended for use by a sailmaker or carpenter, this 13-inch-long hammer includes a turned head some 6¼ inches in length. Though used at some time the mallet remains in good condition.

Frame saws like the whalebone example [136] in the Museum fashioned by Robinson could be used for small jobs on shipboard. In addition, this 13½ by 10½ inch tool could easily have been used by Robinson or other scrimshanders in the preparation of wood, bone, ivory, and other materials.

A specialized woodworking tool is the cooper's croze. Semicircular in shape, the croze was in reality a type of plane used to cut the head grooves in barrels and casks. As casks were assembled on shipboard, some fine adjustments in fitting the heads might require the services of a croze. Josiah Robinson's example [136] is constructed of thick slabs of whalebone with a metal cutter blade imbedded in the adjustable post. The curved fence measures 7⅝ inches in diameter, while the vertical post is some 8 inches in length.

Other examples of carpentering or coopering tools made by scrimshanders include an ivory marking gauge [136] with bronze insets along its eight-inch stem. The sliding ivory fence features a bronze set screw. On the other hand, whalebone, not ivory, is employed in the construction of another carpenter's implement, the square. The perpendicular arms of this tool, graduated in inches, measure 13¹⁄₁₆ and 12⅛ inches respectively.

Boring tools like augers were in constant use on shipboard. A wide range of jobs, from refastening a damaged whaleboat to effecting repairs in the master's cabin, required the use of au-

135. Wood and whalebone lathe is believed to have belonged to scrimshander Josiah Robinson, 28¾ in. (73.0 cm.). *Source:* Harold H. Kynett, 41.288.1-3

137 (center). Auger with whale tooth handle from ship *Siam,* 9¼ in. (23.5 cm.). *Source:* Charles E. White, 39.2045

136. Whalebone replaces wood – scrimshaw carpenter's tools: clockwise from top, frame saw, 13½ x 10½ in. (34.3 x 26.7 cm.); large mallet, 13 in. (33.0 cm.); cooper's croze, 8 x 7⅝ in. (20.3 x 19.4 cm.); auger bit brace, 6⅜ in. (16.2 cm.); and ivory marking gauge, 8 15/16 in. (22.7 cm.). *Sources:* Harold H. Kynett, 41.302, 41.285, 41.289; New England Savings Bank, 39.875; Museum purchase, 52.87

gers. A scrimshander tapped what was probably an abundant source of whalebone to fashion a bit brace [136] for an auger bit. For the swivel knob handle a polished piece of whale ivory was used. Unfortunately, the rigors of everyday use cost the piece its lower shaft.

An auger with a bit of documentation is part of the collection too. This piece [137], with a manufactured metal bit, incorporates a whale tooth as a handle. Engraved on this ivory grip is the following: "SHIP SIAM/1858/NEW LONDON." The *Siam*, built as a packet in 1847, was, by 1858, based in New London, Connecticut. A large vessel, the 727-ton ship was employed on the New London to Honolulu run, probably carrying cargoes of whale oil and baleen home. As Mary Stark's experience aboard the *B.F. Hoxie* proved, these long voyages afforded both the time and materials necessary for scrimshaw work. Thus this auger was probably made by a *Siam* crewman during an 1858 run between Hawaii and home.

138. Sailmaker's gear includes ivory seam rubber with turned handle, 4¾ in. (12.1 cm.); whalebone example with faceted grip, 5¼ in. (13.3 cm.); and work box from Nantucket dated 1830, 7 x 3⅜ in. (17.8 x 8.6 cm.). *Sources:* Mrs. Charles H. Martin, 47.1616; Fred J. Smith, 63.378; Mrs. Raynham Townshend, 47.1476

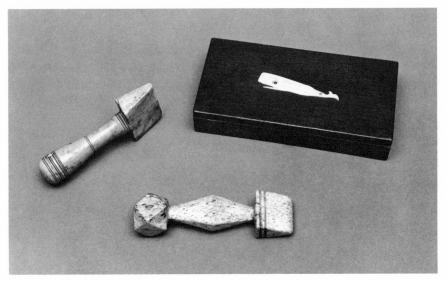

Seam rubbers, those wedge-shaped hand tools designed to crease sail canvas to insure a good seam, are found in a variety of materials, including wood, bone, and ivory. Used in sail lofts ashore, these creasers were also needed by a ship's own sailmaker in repairing old sails and fashioning new ones. Their small size, averaging about five inches, enabled scrimshanders to produce these pieces out of whalebone or ivory. The faceted cube design furnishes the handle knob on a whalebone seam rubber [138]. The shaft of this piece is carved in the shape of a multifaceted diamond, while the working head has the characteristic triangular shape.

An ivory specimen [138] displays the now familiar turning observed in other utilitarian items. This decorative feature in no way detracts from the functional qualities of this particular seam rubber.

John Howland, a nineteenth-century sailmaker, would have used just such an item in his trade. His work box [138], now in the Seaport collection, contains a variety of sailmaker's equipment, including needles, bone bodkins, and a shuttle, also of bone. This seven-inch-long wooden box exhibits some additional evidence of the scrimshander's art in the form of a carved sperm whale. Attached to the box lid, this ivory whale bears the inscription: "John Howland Nantucket/Sailmaker 1830." With Nantucket still a major whaling port in 1830, it is easy to imagine how Howland's box came to be so decorated.

Part of the job of a whaleship's officer, usually the first mate, was to keep the vessel's logbook. A record of the ship's whaling fortunes was an integral part of any such log. Many whaleship logbooks bear inked imprints of whales as a means of recording kills. Carved stamps of wood, ivory, bone, or various combinations of these materials were produced for use with logs. The stamp base would be carved in the shape of a whale, and sometimes separate stamps were made for sperm whales and

139. Carved whale stamps combine wood base with ivory handle. Left to right, a pair of sperm whale stamps with carved floral pattern handles measure 3⅜ in. (8.6 cm.) and 2½ in. (6.3 cm.). An intricate geometric pattern decorates the handle of another whale stamp, 3⅜ in. (8.6 cm.). *Source:* Charles E. White, 39.1901, 39.1904, 39.1903

right or bowhead whales. Oftentimes a blank area was left on the stamp in order that the whale's yield in barrels of oil might be recorded. The all too common occurrence of losing a whale was often noted using a stamp depicting only the escaping creature's flukes.

One writer has stated that the carving of these whale images on the stamps was the closest the scrimshander came to the practice, found in some native cultures, of carving magical symbols.[23] It seems unlikely, however, that the creator of a whale stamp, often the ship's master, ever thought of his handiwork in these terms.

The Museum collection numbers close to two dozen whale stamps. Most are wood with ivory or whalebone handles, and nearly all depict the sperm whale. A pair of these whale stamps [139] share a similar carved floral design in their ivory handles. An ornate geometric pattern reminiscent of the carvings of some Pacific island cultures covers the ivory handle of another example [139].

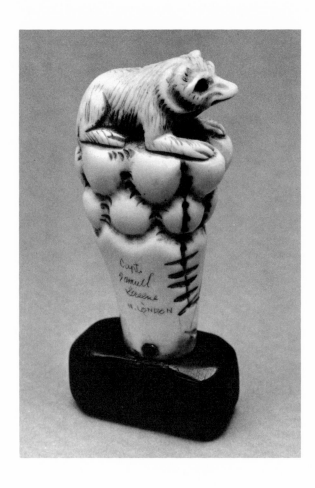

140. An unidentified animal crouches atop an ivory and wood whale stamp carved by whaling master Samuel Greene, 4½ in. (11.4 cm.). *Source:* Mrs. Raynham Townshend, 47.1447

While there is the possibility that these three stamps have a New London connection, there is no doubt about the origin of another piece. The ivory handle of a small sperm whale stamp [140] is carved in the shape of an animal, variously described as a frog or fox, seated atop a rocky pedestal. The identity of the creature is less important than the fact that the piece is engraved "Capt./Samuel/Greene/N. LONDON." Greene (1815-1898) commanded a number of New London and New Bedford whalers, including the *Neptune, Morrison,* and *George & Mary* from the 1840s through the 1860s. Greene appears to have been most active in New London whaling during the 1840s, suggesting that this 4½-inch-tall stamp dates to that period.

It is obvious that the range of utilitarian items was bounded only by the inherent physical limitations of the scrimshander's materials and his own imagination and craftsmanship. Many dozens of items have gone unmentioned due to necessary space limitations; however, the many and various objects described should suggest the incredible diversity of this art in general and of the Museum's collection in particular.

Chapter 5 *Scrimshaw Collecting Today*

IT IS probably safe to venture that scrimshaw has never been so popular among collectors as it is now. More and more people seem to be turning their attention to this nautical art; and many appear willing to invest considerable sums in pursuit of the whaleman's handiwork. The reasons for this interest are as varied as the individual collectors: some view scrimshaw, like other collectibles, as an investment and hedge against inflation; others acquire pieces as part of a broader interest in American folk art; still others consider scrimshaw valid evidence in documenting one particular phase of our nation's history.

As noted earlier in this work the most obvious result of this heightened interest can be seen in scrimshaw's performance in the marketplace. It is not unknown for certain individual items to bring upward of $10,000 at auction; indeed the current record for a single piece is the $40,000 paid in 1982 for one of Frederick Myrick's "*Susan*'s teeth." Yet for all the excitement and money involved there seems to be some lack of understanding of the factors that determine the relative importance of a piece.

Collecting: What to Look for

Certainly visual appeal is basic no matter what the collector's motive. But beyond first impressions are other considerations that should be taken into account.

Complementing the aesthetic quality of a piece, for instance, should be the technical competence of the work, especially in the ship portraits and whaling scenes. For example, is the rig of the vessel correct? Whalers, often rigged as ships or barks, were built for capacity and not speed. Their usually broad-beamed hulls did not require the lofty rigs carried by the more stream-lined clippers or sailing packets of the day. Are the whaleboats correct? American whaleboats carried six men, three rowing to starboard, two to port, and a boatsteerer manning the large steering sweep astern. The harpooner would exchange his oar for a harpoon as the boat approached a whale, thus temporarily reducing the craft's power to four oars. It is possible that some foreign whalers might have utilized a somewhat different arrangement of men and oars, but the six-man boat as described was standard in the American whale fishery. Is the cutting-in operation correct? Most American whalers cut in on the starboard side, though the English were known to use the port side of the vessel for this purpose. The point to be made is that while the scrimshander might lack certain artistic skills he was nonetheless a knowledgeable seaman who understood his trade and was thus less likely to commit purely technical errors than someone unfamiliar with whaling.

Built-in documentation adds greatly to an item's historical importance, which in turn is reflected in its marketplace appeal. Just as a signed Rembrandt is considered more valuable than a work "in the style of" the master, so too is a signed piece of

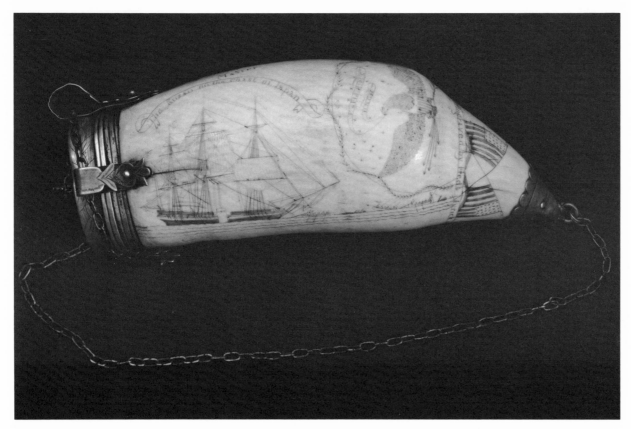

141. View of a *"Susan*'s tooth" engraved by Frederick Myrick "February the 23rd 1829," showing the vessel cutting in. The silver work is possibly unique on a Myrick tooth, 7½ in. (19.0 cm.). Courtesy of The Dietrich Brothers Americana Corporation, Philadelphia. Photograph by Will Brown.

scrimshaw considered more important than an unsigned item of comparable quality. Because most scrimshaw is the work of anonymous artists, the occasional signed example is unusual and worthy of note. Based on the identity of the scrimshander, it is sometimes possible to determine the probable date of the piece, the name of the vessel upon which it was fashioned, and other data. Engraved vessel names, dates, and identifiable locales, found either together or singly on scrimshaw items, are other forms of documentation that increase the historical significance of an example, and hence its desirability to collectors.

Written documentation, in the form of letters, logbook entries, journals, and similar evidence, which corroborates the verbal history of a piece, is certainly valuable in placing an item in the proper historical context. Sally Smith's voluminous *Ohio* journal is a splendid example of this type of primary documentation. A related factor is the provenance of a piece, that is, its history of ownership down through the years. An item whose complete history can be traced is fairly uncommon. By the same token a piece of scrimshaw once owned by a well-known individual can generate special interest.

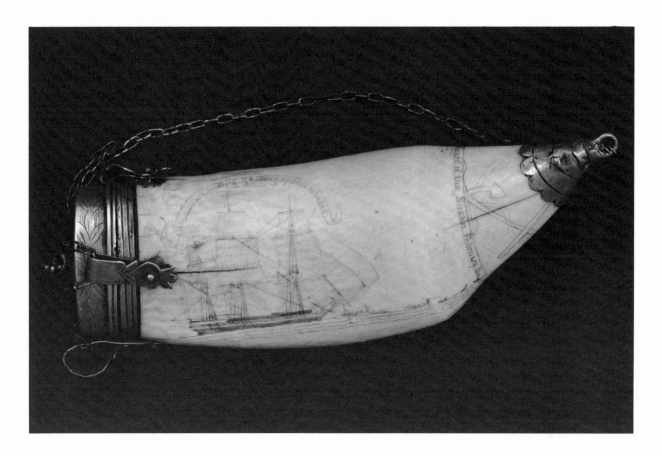

142. Reverse of "*Susan*'s tooth" showing the ship "boiling & killing sperm whales," 7¹/₂ in. (19.0 cm.). Courtesy of The Dietrich Brothers Americana Corporation, Philadelphia. Photograph by Will Brown.

Finally, the physical condition of a scrimshaw item has a bearing on its market value and, depending on the nature of any damage, its historical value as well.

Do these factors really count in determining the importance of a piece of scrimshaw? Consider the case of one of Myrick's "*Susan*'s teeth" [141, 142], engraved during the 1826-1829 voyage of the Nantucket whaleship *Susan*. Excluding the exquisite silverwork, unusual even for a Myrick piece, it's easy to see that this scrimshander's artistic gifts were of a high order. A recent report, so far unconfirmed, held that an example of Myrick's

penmanship from his schooldays had surfaced on Nantucket and that it indicated considerable artistic talent at an early age.

A close look at the two renderings of the *Susan*, one a cutting-in view [141], the other with the ship trying out the blubber [142], is enough to convince anyone that Myrick understood the workings of a whaleship from reef points to dolphin striker. Equally accurate are his views of the whale hunt, correct down to the number and placement of men and oars in each whaleboat.

Built-in documentation abounds on this piece, not the least

· 133 ·

of which is the fact that the tooth is signed "Engraved by Fred^k Myrick on board of the Susan February the 23rd 1829." A banner floating above one of the ship's portraits locates the *Susan* "on the Coast of Japan." Myrick goes on to note the ship's homeport of Nantucket and her master, Frederick Swain. A more complete job of documentation is hard to imagine, especially on so early an example.

Research by Everett U. Crosby of Nantucket and others has determined that Myrick produced a series of these teeth on this whaling voyage. Depending on whom you ask, the number of "*Susan*'s teeth" ranges from perhaps twelve to twenty-two.[1]

It is clear that these factors play an enormous role is determining the importance of Myrick's teeth; and these same considerations are equally valid in evaluating other scrimshaw as well.

Research: Where to Look

The importance of historical research to the scrimshaw collector should not be underestimated. Only by understanding the realities of the American whaling industry in general and the life of the whaleman in particular can scrimshaw be placed in proper historical perspective. Many academic and museum libraries, as well as larger public libraries, offer a selection of works describing nineteenth-century American whaling. Learn about this business, the techniques and equipment used, and the conditions of employment.

More detailed information regarding specific vessels, masters, and voyages is available in a number of printed sources. Alexander Starbuck's 1878 *History of the American Whale Fishery,* for example, lists most American whaling voyages from the late eighteenth century through 1876. An addendum covers the remaining half century of American whaling activity. Special

annual vessel listings such as the U. S. Government's *Merchant Vessels of the U. S.,* American Lloyd's *Registry of American and Foreign Shipping,* and the American Shipmasters' Association's *Record of American and Foreign Shipping* offer additional data. Detailed nineteenth-century customs house records, compiled and published by the W. P. A. during the late 1930s and early 1940s, are available at certain research and marine libraries and contain a wealth of information about specific vessels.

Primary research materials like whaleship logbooks, official or personal journals kept on shipboard, crew lists, letters, and business records are all potential sources of information regarding particular whalemen and vessels.

These sources, both published and primary, were indispensable in the writing of this monograph. They can serve the student or collector of scrimshaw equally well in many cases by helping to build documentation for a piece. Though it may require a bit of time and patience it is time well spent—and can be a good deal of fun as well.

Protective Legislation

As a result of the threatened extinction of certain species of animals, the United States Congress passed several pieces of legislation of profound significance for collectors of scrimshaw.[2] The Marine Mammals Protection Act of 21 October 1972 prohibited the taking or importation of certain endangered marine mammals or their by-products. Such animals, including whales and walruses, and their by-products taken before this date were exempt from these prohibitions.

The Endangered Species Act of 1973 broadened the prohibitions by making it illegal to import, export, or ship and sell in interstate commerce any of the protected species or their by-products. Scrimshaw and other whale by-products held before the 28 December 1973 enactment of this law were *not* exempted, in effect outlawing all interstate sale of scrimshaw.

In 1976 this law was amended to allow limited interstate commerce and/or exportation of scrimshaw. The Secretary of Commerce made available three-year exemption certificates, issued between August 1976 and August 1977, enabling scrimshaw owners and collectors to buy and sell across state lines. Very few people took advantage of these certificates, which were subsequently made renewable for another three years. Administration and enforcement of the provisions of these acts related to scrimshaw is currently in the hands of the National Marine Fisheries Service.

Despite an outcry from scrimshaw collectors and contemporary practitioners of this type of art, no amendment has been forthcoming. To the best of our knowledge at this writing, importation, exportation, and interstate shipment and sale of scrimshaw items without a valid exemption certificate is prohibited. Some states have legislation controlling or prohibiting intrastate sale of scrimshaw, so it would be best to learn the pertinent regulations before becoming involved in collecting.

Scrimshaw: Its Care and Feeding

Bone, ivory, baleen, and many other materials used by scrimshanders are organic and thus susceptible to damage due to a number of factors. Like wood, ivory and bone will slowly dry out with age, leading to checking along the direction of the grain. Checking serves as a safety valve for the inherent stresses in a piece of bone or ivory, and no amount of restorative effort will ever replace the cellular moisture loss causing this condition.

While nothing can completely stop this degenerative process, quite a bit can be done to retard drying and thus extend the life of the item. Not surprisingly, heat is a major culprit in the premature damaging of bone and ivory artifacts. Therefore scrimshaw should be kept clear of radiators, wood stoves, fireplaces, and similar heat sources. As bone and ivory dry they become more brittle, so use care in handling scrimshaw.

Direct sunlight poses a twofold threat: it can generate destructive heat and at the same time fade decorative inks. Beware of other strong ultraviolet sources like standard or unfiltered fluorescent lights, which can also promote the fading of inking pigments.

The Museum regularly receives requests for advice on how best to clean scrimshaw. It is almost always recommended that nothing be done to a piece of scrimshaw lest irreparable damage occur. Primary among the dangers of cleaning such items is the loss of inking. Some of the pigments used are water-soluble, and an attempt at "cleaning" might prove disastrously successful. In most instances the stains and smears on a piece are considered as much a part of the history of the item as the maker's original engraving effort. So think twice before undertaking any steps to clean a piece.

Baleen too becomes brittle with age. Splitting along the grain is not uncommon. A special problem with this material is the threat of pest damage. Insects, probably beetles of some type, have feasted on a sizable percentage of baleen scrimshaw items found in both public and private collections. Busks, ditty boxes, and other pieces composed largely of this particular substance are fair game to voracious vermin, so regular inspection of these items is a good idea.

Finally, in handling scrimshaw of any type be certain your hands are clean or, if possible, wear soft gloves to avoid dirt and oil stains as well as a loss of inking. Proper care of scrimshaw comes down to a mixture of caution and common sense. Following such simple guidelines will enable us all to preserve and pass on those artifacts we have had the good fortune to acquire.

Reproductions and Fakes: When Is a Tooth Not a Tooth?

Partly as a result of scrimshaw's increasing popularity, and in view of the limited supply of available pieces, a number of authorized museum reproductions have appeared over the past few years. A leader in the production and marketing of reproduction scrimshaw is Artek, Inc., of Antrim, New Hampshire, which currently supplies a line of "polymer ivory" teeth, tusks, panbone, and other items.

Several maritime museums, among them the Peabody Museum of Salem, the Nantucket Whaling Museum, and Mystic Seaport Museum, cooperate in this venture by allowing examples from their scrimshaw collections to be replicated accurately in this synthetic material. For those who cannot find or afford original scrimshaw items, these reproductions offer an alternative, capturing as they do much of the feel and aesthetic quality of the genuine article.

To avoid confusion with real scrimshaw, one or more recessed mold marks are incorporated on each piece. Besides the Artek name, the word "reproduction" or "replica" is included and, in the case of museum-owned scrimshaw, the initials of the institution holding the original piece, e.g., "PMS," "NWM," or "MS." These molded marks are normally located on the underside of the piece, or near or within the cavity in the case of a tooth.

In recent years some of these fine reproductions have appeared on the antiques market with their mold marks intentionally obliterated. On several occasions the Museum has been offered a chance to acquire a fine whale tooth, only to discover it to be an Artek copy of our own "Shoal of Sperm Whales" piece [11]. Such tampering continues and is a source of concern to both Artek and the museums involved.

A more ominous development is the flood of unmarked plastic scrimshaw from England evident in recent years. Molded of a polystyrene material,[3] these teeth, tusks, panbones, ostrich eggs, and tortoise shells are apparently produced by a group in Britain collectively known for marketing purposes as Juratone Ltd. Unlike the Artek reproductions, these curious specimens employ a combination of real and fictitious vessel names along with other data and designs copied from published illustrations of authentic scrimshaw. These pieces are in no way marked to indicate their manufactured origin, leading people both here and abroad to pay considerable sums for what they believe to be real scrimshaw. Ironically, one of the most popular of these fakes is a large walrus tusk [143] depicting the Seaport's own *Charles W. Morgan*. Over one dozen examples of this particular fake have been discovered since 1979, and undoubtedly scores more have been purchased by the unsuspecting at flea markets and antique shows. Thus far the overall method of marketing these pieces, which often includes an "elderly widow from New Bedford" as part of their provenance, has largely eluded detection.

A number of tests can aid in the detection of polymer "scrimshaw," both Artek reproductions and these Juratone examples. Under long-wave ultraviolet light, real bone and ivory appear bright white, while polymer pieces so tested do not react. Another nondestructive test involves the use of moderate power (about 30x) magnification. Tiny, perfectly round air

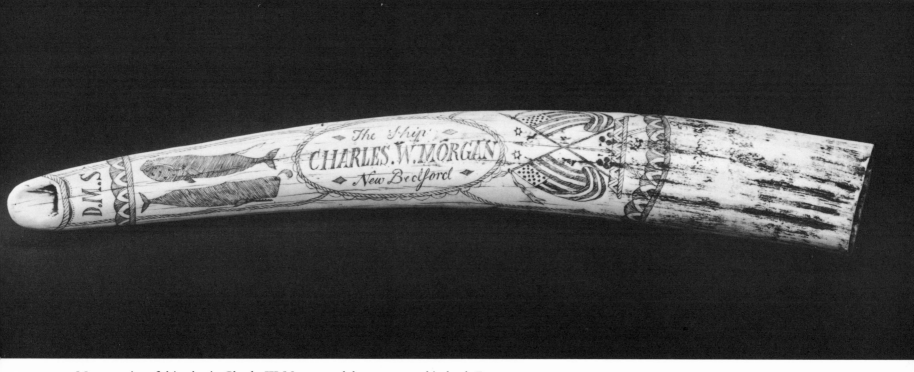

143. Many copies of this plastic *Charles W. Morgan* tusk have appeared in both Europe and North America since 1979, 22¼ in. (56.5 cm.). *Source:* Anonymous, 80.30

bubbles, a result of the liquid molding process, can be seen on the surface, especially near the ends of the piece.

Recently Constance P. Ramstedt, an antique substance analyst from California, determined that the polymer in Artek reproductions will hold an electrostatic charge, while real bone and ivory will not.[4] The author recently submitted a Juratone piece to this same test and found the results to be the same. The plastic piece accepted the electrostatic charge, achieved in this case by vigorously rubbing with a piece of corduroy material, and was able to attract a small scrap of tissue paper. A real tooth similarly tested failed to hold any charge.

This test, though simple to perform in the field, is compli-cated by such variables as humidity levels, possible use of anti-static coatings on plastic pieces, and the type of material used to generate the static charge. The one thing that can definitely be ascertained from this test is that if a piece holds an electrostatic charge it is *not* bone or ivory.

The much-publicized "hot needle" test can work *if* the needle is hot enough, *if* the needle point is the right size, and *if* the polymer is homogeneous throughout the piece. Bone or ivory will not melt or smell, but polymer material should when touched with a hot needle. If trying this test, be sure to use an inconspicuous spot on the piece such as within the cavity of a tooth.

Modern Work

The practice of scrimshaw declined by the beginning of this century, paralleling the fortunes of the American whaling industry. Despite the virtual collapse of this industry by the 1920s, some people continued the whaleman's art, most notably in the engraving of sperm whale teeth. As noted in an earlier chapter, the style of this work took on a decidedly more romantic flavor than that employed by the nineteenth-century whaleman. This was especially true in the depictions of vessels, whaling, and the whaleman himself. Some of these twentieth-century artists signed their work and some did not.

One of the more prolific was William Perry of New Bedford, who worked from perhaps the 1920s into the 1960s. Perry frequently used lithographs and other illustrations as models for his scenes, into which he often salted his initials. A "w" might be found in a cloud, while a "P" could turn up on a wave

or perhaps lurking in the rigging of a ship. The Seaport currently has nine identified Perry pieces, tusks and teeth alike [144], plus two "probables."

Despite the obstacles posed by protective legislation, some artists continue to produce engraved whale teeth and other items. William Gilkerson is one of the most talented and best-known practitioners of this art. Like many of his contemporaries, he signs and sometimes dates his work, thus avoiding confusion with nineteenth-century pieces.

Less scrupulous individuals are engraving whale teeth and similar items and are misrepresenting them as nineteenth-century scrimshaw. Apparently this is not a new problem, for as early as the 1940s there was an awareness among collectors and museums alike that newly engraved scrimshaw was on the market, purporting to be old.[5]

England, the source of so much fake plastic scrimshaw, appears to be one of the centers of this related trade as well. One

144. An example of modern engraving by William Perry of New Bedford, 7 in. (17.8 cm.). *Source:* Dr. Ier J. Manwaring, 59.1129

145. A genuine fake: the tooth is real but the "old" engraving is modern, 7 in. (17.8 cm.). *Source:* Collection of R. J. Narkis

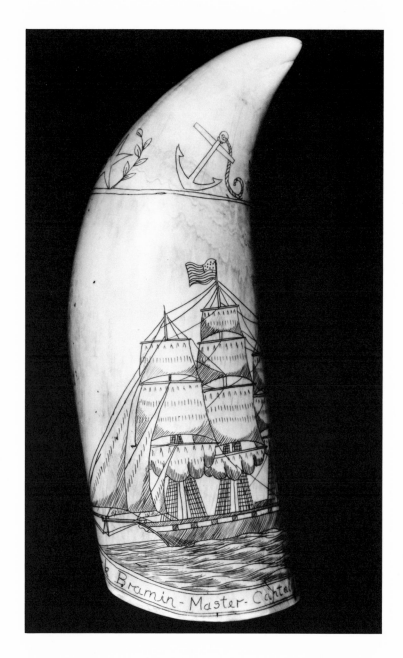

individual wrote telling us of his tooth [145], purchased in London, done by Captain Butts of the Mystic whaler *Bramin*. Of course, the piece was faked using bits of information gleaned from an illustration of our pair of teeth [see color plate opp. p. 81] brought home by Captain Butts of New Bedford in 1851. It is an impressive-looking piece, to be sure, but every bit as fake as the plastic *Charles W. Morgan* tusk.

These so-called "real" fakes cannot be tested using the methods devised for detecting plastic pieces. However, besides obvious errors in the engraved data, the surface of an item, especially a whale tooth, can offer some clues. Whale teeth were prepared by hand on shipboard and often exhibit telltale scrape marks along the grain, the result of patient effort with knife or file. Modern fakes on real teeth are often smoothed and polished using power equipment, thus avoiding such characteristic marks.[6] Examine a piece carefully, especially with raking light shining down its length, and see if the surface is much too uniform and smooth. Check the engraving work as well. Is it too consistent and well defined?

In a marketplace where the warning *caveat emptor*, "let the buyer beware," is still valid, there is no entirely foolproof means of easily detecting fakes. The preceding suggestions are just that – suggestions – and should not be followed blindly in every case. It bears repeating, however, that the prospective collector would be well advised to learn as much as possible about whaling and its artistic offshoot, scrimshaw. Careful examination of scrimshaw items, both as illustrated in published works and as displayed in museums, will enable one to gain a much better feel for this handiwork of the mariner and whaleman.

APPENDICES

Appendix 1   *Scrimshanders Represented in the Collection*

Attributions are based on one or more of the following: provenance, family history, comparison with signed pieces, and supplementary documentation.

A., B.
  41.42; tooth
A., T.
  57.114; tooth
Abbott, Henry R.
  70.317; tooth
Albro, T. L.
  81.40; tooth
B., M.
  54.1601. 32; ring
B., W.
  39.2117; seam rubber
Bayley, C.
  41.370; cane
Bly, Isaac
  82.1.2; busk
Bradford, Captain Benjamin W.
  82.2; tooth
Burdett, Edward
  56.172; tooth
Carlson, Francis
  43.336; cane
Chapin, Sila[s]
  47.1397; busk
Clark, B. H.
  47.1376; tooth
Clark, James
  39.1752; gavel
Clift, Captain William
  36.25; ditty box

D., E.
  64.1222; needle case
Dodge, Ephraim J.
  61.1111; baleen
F., L. D.
  39.1770; tooth
F., P.
  37.38; cane
Foster, Washington
  39.2077; club
Gl., E.
  39.1741; tooth
Greene, Captain Samuel
  47.1447; whale stamp
H., N. W.
  39.1776; tooth
Harris, Albert
  39.883; busk
  39.886; busk
Haskins
  47.1428; walrus tusk
Hewit, Charles
  39.1915; busk
Holmes, Captain Joseph W.
  36.36; ivory slab
Howland, John
  47.1476; sailmaker's box
Huggins, Samuel, Jr.
  39.859; tooth
I., J. I.
  39.1960; panbone
Ike
  39.1744; tooth
Jones, H. W.
  65.1029; busk
K., H. B.
  47.1378; tooth

K., J.
  48.974; fid
Kenyon, S., attributed to
  58.949; fid
Knowles, John
  47.1417; spoon
L., M. R.
  39.857; tooth
L., W. M.
  39.1886; fid
M., E. M.
  39.880; busk
M., J.
  39.1754-1755; teeth
Marshall, John
  70.321; tooth
Martin, James
  47.1348; club
McKenzie, Daniel, Jr., attributed to
  81.64.19; tooth
Montague, James
  39.1869; walrus tusk
  39.1876; walrus tusk
Morgan, Captain Stephen
  39.382; dipper bowl
  Attributed to:
  39.383; creamer
  39.384; sugar bowl
  39.385; sugar bowl
  39.386; bowl
  39.1927; creamer
  39.1928; sugar bowl
  45.4; dipper bowl
P.,E. (or T., E.)
  57.870; walrus tusk
Perry, William
  39.1724-1725; teeth

Appendix 2   *Vessels Represented in the Collection*

Acushnet, American whaleship
  39.1723-1724; teeth (modern work)
Adventure, British whaling bark
  56.173; tooth
  78.144; tooth
Arethusa, British frigate
  52.89.3; tooth
B. F. Hoxie, American ship
  48.1043; busk
Boston, American warship (?)
  41.435; tooth
Charles W. Morgan, American whaling bark
  78.253; cane
Columbia, American whaleship
  39.1872; fid
Constitution, U. S. Navy frigate
  39.1746; tooth
  41.367; cane
  49.1253; tooth
  52.89.3; tooth
Droits, La, French warship
  52.89.3; tooth
Emmeline, American schooner
  39.2077; club
Epervier, British naval brig
  49.1253; tooth
Friends, American whaleship
  56.172; tooth
General Washington, American brig
  47.1368; tooth (modern work)
Globe, American steamboat
  75.6 ab; porpoise jaw
Guerrière, British frigate
  39.1746; tooth
Isabella, American whaling bark
  57.870; walrus tusk

Java, British frigate
  49.1253; tooth
  52.89.3; tooth
Jeanette, American steam bark
  76.8-9; walrus tusks
John Coggeshall, American whaleship
  81.40; tooth
Loper, British brig
  52.89.3; tooth
Macedonian, British frigate
  40.115; tooth
Magnolia, American whaleship
  47.1334; gauge stick
Maria, American whaling bark
  55.463; tooth
Maury, American schooner
  59.1125; tooth (modern work ?)
Mechanic, American whaleship
  55.1037; tooth
Medina, British ship
  57.114; tooth
Mentor, American whaleship
  39.1752; gavel
Mercury, American whaleship
  39.1782; tooth powder horn
  39.2047; blubber hook
Morning Star, American whaling bark
  47.1348; club
Neptune, American whaleship
  39.1729; tooth
  39.1734; tooth
Ocean, Norwegian ship
  41.631.14; letter opener
Ohio, American whaling bark
  41.306-307; teeth (modern work)
  41.631.14; letter opener

Otter, sloop
  81.13.3; tooth (modern work)
Panderson (?), brig
  47.1380; tooth
Peacock, U. S. Navy ship-sloop
  49.1253; tooth
Pennsylvania, U. S. Navy ship of the line
  79.84; tooth
President, American whaleship
  39.859; tooth
Roamer, whaleship (?)
  47.1366; tooth
Rochester, British whaling bark
  39.1802; tooth
Sea Hound, American whaleship (?)
  39.1732; tooth
Siam, American ship
  39.2045; auger
Spartan, American whaleship
  47.1346-1347; walrus tusks
Superior, American whaling bark
  61.1111; baleen
Swift, American whaleship
  39.1873; walrus tusk
Triton, American whaleship
  47.1429; spoon
  70.321; tooth
United States, U. S. Navy frigate
  40.115; tooth
Warren Hastings, British ship
  57.114; tooth
William Tell, American whaleship
  56.172; tooth
Yorktown, U. S. Navy ship-sloop
  59.1125; tooth (modern work?)

Appendix 3 *People and Places Represented in the Collection*

A

Agriculture, figure of
81.64.22; busk
Alexander II, Czar
39.1740; tooth
Alwilda, the female pirate
47.1345; walrus tusk
57.870; walrus tusk
America, figure of
57.704; walrus tusk
Apia, Samoa
39.1873; walrus tusk

B

Banks, General Nathaniel P.
57.702;walrus tusk
Beads Harbour, Canada
39.1348; club
Blake, Mary Elizabeth
47.1463; pie crimper
Bonaparte, Napoleon
39.1797; tooth
Boston, Massachusetts
39.1732; tooth
55.1038; tooth
59.1126; tooth
70.317; tooth
British East India Company
57.114; tooth
Byron, Lord
74.691; tooth

C

Callao, Peru
39.1752; gavel
41.367; cane

Campbell, Fanny, the female pirate
39.1804; tooth
Castle of Fame
41.42; tooth
Champlain, Lake, Battle of
41.412; tooth
Chile, Republic of
40.118; cane
Claxton, Commodore Alexander, U.S.N.
41.367; cane
Columbia, figure of
57.702; walrus tusk
57.704;walrus tusk
57.705; walrus tusk
Crozet Islands, Indian Ocean
39.2077; club
Cupid
81.64.22; busk

D

Daggett, Captain Henry
55.1037; tooth
Diana, figure of
39.1782; tooth powder horn

E

Earle, Captain James
78.253; cane
Easter Island
39.1752; gavel
Erie, Lake, Battle of
41.411; tooth
Eve, figure of
36.54; tooth

F

Fanny Campbell, the female pirate
39.1804; tooth
Flores, Azores
41.631.14; letter opener
Foote, Commodore Andrew H., U.S.N.
57.702; walrus tusk
French Rock, South Pacific Ocean
39.1873; walrus tusk
81.40; tooth

G

Galápagos Islands
39.1752; gavel
39.1873; walrus tusk
Grant, General Ulysses S.
45.266; walrus tusk
57.705; walrus tusk
Guinea, Africa
47.1352; tooth

H

Hamlet
36.54; tooth
Harris, Charlotte M.
39.883; busk
Havana, Cuba
41.367; cane
Hope, figure of
39.1798; tooth
Howland, John
47.1476; sailmaker's box
Howland, Mary
47.1464; pie crimper
Hudson Bay, Canada
47.1348; club

I

Infant drummer
47.1354; tooth

J

Jack Tar
47.1373; tooth
Jones, John Paul
73.446; walrus tusk
Jordan, South Carolina
43.336; cane
Juan Fernandez Islands
41.367; cane
Justice, figure of
49.1247; tooth
55.1037; tooth

K

Kenyon, Adelaide
81.86.1; tooth
Knowles, John
47.1417; spoon

L

Liberty, figure of
39.1747; tooth
39.1775; tooth
41.435; tooth
57.702; walrus tusk
57.705; walrus tusk
73.431; tooth
Lima, Peru
39.1752; gavel
Lincoln, Abraham
39.1740; tooth
57.704; walrus tusk
Lyme, Connecticut
39.1915; busk

M

McCarty, Captain
56.173; tooth
78.144; tooth

McDonough, Commodore Thomas, U.S.N.
41.412; tooth
McKenzie, Adeline
81.64.19; tooth
McKenzie, Alexander
81.64.19; tooth
McKenzie, Captain Daniel
81.64.19; tooth
McKenzie, Daniel, Jr.
81.64.19; tooth
McKenzie, Mary (I)
81.64.19; tooth
McKenzie, Mary (II)
81.64.19; tooth
McKenzie, Nancy
81.64.19; tooth
McKenzie, Phebe
81.64.19; tooth
Marsh, William H.
47.1354; tooth
Marshall Islands
39.1752; gavel
Mombassa, West Africa
47.1352; tooth
Mystic, Connecticut
39.2077; club

N

Nantucket, Massachusetts
47.1346-1347; walrus tusks
47.1464; pie crimper
47.1476; sailmaker's box
Napoleon I
39.1797; tooth
Navigator Islands (Samoa)
39.1873; walrus tusk
Neptune, figure of
57.702; tusk
New Bedford, Massachusetts
39.1732; tooth
39.1873; walrus tusk
39.1951; pie crimper
47.1348; club
47.1602; whale stamp
55.463; tooth

59.1128; tooth
73.445; walrus tusk
81.64.23; busk
82.1.2; busk
New Guinea
39.1752; gavel
New London, Connecticut
39.1752; gavel
39.1872; fid
39.2045; auger
47.1447; whale stamp
56.172; tooth
New York City
39.860; tooth
41.367; cane
56.172; tooth
New Zealand
39.1752; gavel
39.1873; walrus tusk
Newport, Rhode Island
81.40; tooth
Norfolk, Virginia
41.367; cane

O

Old Nick, the devil
47.1428; walrus tusk

P

Patterson, Sadie
39.1951; pie crimper
Payta, Peru
41.367; cane
Pernambuco (Recife), Brazil
39.1752; gavel
Perry, Commodore Oliver H., U.S.N.
41.411; tooth
41.436; tooth
Peru
39.1802; tooth
Pilgrims
57.702; walrus tusk
Pilgrim monument
57.702; walrus tusk

Plenty, figure of
47.1352; tooth
55.1037; tooth
Provincetown, Massachusetts
52.40; panbone
Puná, Ecuador
41.367; cane

Q

Queen Charlotte Islands
70.321; tooth

R

Rarotonga Island, South Pacific Ocean
39.1802; tooth
Repulse Bay, Canada
47.1348; club
Rider, Captain William
56.880; cane
Rio de Janeiro, Brazil
41.367; cane
Robinson, Lucy
41.297.1; pie crimper

S

Salem, Massachusetts (?)
39.1787; tooth
Samoa
47.1364; tooth
Sandwich Islands (Hawaii)
39.1752; gavel

Scott, General Winfield
57.704; walrus tusk
Seychelles, Indian Ocean
39.1802; tooth
Sherman, General William T.
57.705; walrus tusk
Smith, Captain Frederick H.
41.294; picture frame
41.631.14; letter opener
41.632.16; pipe bowl
Smith, Sarah G., "Sallie"
41.294; picture frame
41.296; fan
41.628; work box
41.632.2; pie crimper
41.632.6; butter knife
41.632.17; tatting shuttle
Spicer, Captain John O.
55.951; picture frame
Stonington, Connecticut
36.113; ruler
Sunday Isle (Raoul), Pacific Ocean
39.1873; walrus tusk

T

Tahiti
39.1752; gavel
Talcahuano, Chile
41.367; cane
Taylor, General Zachary
47.1357; tooth
Turner, Captain Daniel, U.S.N.
41.367; cane

U

U. S. Capitol Building
79.84; tooth

V

Valparaiso, Chile
39.1752; gavel
39.1802; tooth
41.367; cane
Vera Cruz, Mexico
41.367; cane

W

Washington, D. C.
45.266; walrus tusk
57.702; walrus tusk
79.84; tooth
Washington, George
39.1720; tooth
39.1747; tooth
39.1791; tooth
39.1798; tooth
45.266; walrus tusk
47.1368; tooth
57.702; walrus tusk
57.704; walrus tusk
59.1126; tooth
Washington, Martha
57.703; walrus tusk
Williams, Mary P.
58.1200c; knitting needle

NOTES

CHAPTER ONE

1. E. Norman Flayderman, *Scrimshaw and Scrimshanders* (New Milford, Conn., 1972), pp. 4-6.
2. Letter in *The Log of Mystic Seaport*, 3, no. 1 (January 1951), p. 11.
3. "Logbook of the Brig *Orion*, Obed Luce Master," 14 March 1821. G. W. Blunt White Library, Mystic Seaport Museum, Log 293.
4. Flayderman, p. 3.
5. Joseph F. Caron, "Scrimshaw and Its Importance as an American Folk Art," Ph.D. dissertation, Illinois State University, 1976, p. 91.
6. Flayderman, p. 28.
7. Robert G. Albion, William A. Baker, and Benjamin W. Labaree, *New England and the Sea* (Middletown, Conn., 1972), p. 116.
8. Walter K. Earle, *Scrimshaw: Folk Art of the Whalers* (Cold Spring Harbor, N.Y.: Whaling Museum Society, Inc., 1957), p. 33.
9. Quoted in Arthur C. Watson, *The Long Harpoon* (New Bedford, Mass., 1929).
10. Flayderman, p. 29.
11. Caron, p. 66.
12. G. Haskins, *Narrative of a Global Whaling Voyage, 1829-1833* (London, 1839). Quoted in Flayderman, p. 10.
13. Flayderman, p. 10.
14. Clifford W. Ashley, *The Yankee Whaler* (Boston, 1926), p. 111.
15. Caron, p. 68.
16. Caron, p. 105.
17. Maurius Barbeau, "Seafaring Folk Art," *Antiques,* 66, no. 1 (July 1954), p. 48.
18. Caron, p. 117.
19. Ashley, p. 112.
20. Earle, p. 20.
21. Caron, p. 65.
22. Flayderman, p. 28.
23. Norbert J. Beihoff, *Ivory Sculpture through the Ages*, Milwaukee Public Museum Publications in History, no. 3 (Milwaukee, 1961), p. 17. Quoted in Flayderman, p. 28.
24. Museum correspondence, John Bockstoce to Richard C. Malley, 19 December 1980.

25. Herman Melville, *Moby-Dick* (New York, 1851), pp. 302-303.
26. Claggett Wilson, "Scrimshaw, the Whaleman's Art," *Antiques,* 46, no. 5 (November 1944), pp. 278-279.
27. Carson I. A. Ritchie, *Modern Ivory Carving* (New York, 1972), p. 54.
28. Wilson, p. 280.
29. Caron, p. 74.

CHAPTER TWO

1. Gertrude E. Noyes, *The Savings Bank of New London* (New London, 1977), pp. 64-66.
2. Museum correspondence, Carl Cutler to Clifford D. Mallory, Sr., 14 October 1938.
3. Museum correspondence, Gerald Fox to W. Douglas McKay, 2 March 1952.

CHAPTER THREE

1. Caron, p. 83.
2. Caron, p. 89.
3. Flayderman, p. 29.
4. Lloyd's *Register of British Shipping*, 1842.
5. Flayderman, p. 106.
6. Museum correspondence, Edouard A. Stackpole to J. Revell Carr, 20 June 1977.
7. Francis A. Olmsted, *Incidents of a Whaling Voyage* (New York, 1841), pp. 146-147.
8. Olmsted, p. 159.
9. Edouard A. Stackpole, *Scrimshaw at Mystic Seaport* (Mystic, Conn., 1958), p. 10.
10. Alexander Starbuck in *History of the American Whale Fishery* (1878) lists Edward Harding as master during the first voyage, 1834-1838.
11. Earle, p. 33.
12. Journal of W. S. Maxfield aboard ship *Niger*, 17 October 1852. Quoted in Emma M. Whiting and Henry B. Hough, *Whaling Wives* (Boston, 1953), p. 71.

13. Earle, p. 27.

14. Ashley, p. 114.

15. Caron, p. 80.

16. Caron, p. 81.

17. Caron, p. 80.

18. Caron, p. 86.

19. For a more complete treatment of these female pirates see Flayderman, pp. 76-79.

20. Mairin Mitchell, *The Maritime History of Russia, 1848-1948* (London, 1949), p. 245.

21. Caron, p. 90. Based on information from Abby Aldrich Rockefeller Folk Art Center, Williamsburg, Virginia.

22. Theodore Roosevelt, *The Naval War of 1812* (New York, 1910), p. 110.

23. Priscilla Sawyer Lord and Daniel J. Foley, *The Folk Arts and Crafts of New England* (Philadelphia, 1965), p. 97.

24. Philip M. Isaacson, *The American Eagle* (Boston, 1975), p. 19.

25. Lord and Foley, p. 97.

26. For comparisons see Flayderman, p. 59.

27. Isaacson, pp. 4-5.

28. William Gilkerson, *The Scrimshander*, rev. ed. (San Francisco, 1978), p. 4.

CHAPTER FOUR

1. Edward L. Daland, "Engraved Types of Scrimshaw," *Antiques*, 28, no. 4 (October 1935), p. 155, note.

2. Quoted in Ashley, p. 144.

3. Caron, p. 77.

4. Letters of Mary R. Stark to Lizzie Stark, April 1855 to January 1856. G. W. Blunt White Library, Mystic Seaport Museum, Coll. VFM 196.

5. Henry S. Stark to Sanford Stark, 8 December 1855. G. W. Blunt White Library, Mystic Seaport Museum, Coll. VFM 196.

6. Quoted in Watson, p. 162.

7. U. S. Navy Department, *Dictionary of American Naval Fighting Ships*, 2 (Washington, D. C., 1963), p. 176.

8. Entries in logs and journals kept by the Smiths while on board these vessels help document a number of the pieces credited to the hand of Captain Smith. These manuscripts are also part of the Museum's collection.

9. "Journal of Sallie G. Smith aboard the Bark *Ohio*, 1875-1878." G. W. Blunt White Library, Mystic Seaport Museum, Log 399.

10. "Journal of Sallie G. Smith aboard the Bark *John P. West*, 1881-1883." G. W. Blunt White Library, Mystic Seaport Museum, Log 78.

11. "Journal of Sallie G. Smith aboard the Bark *Ohio*," 9 January 1878. G. W. Blunt White Library, Mystic Seaport Museum, Log 399.

12. "Journal of Sallie G. Smith aboard the Bark *Ohio*," 20 March 1878. G. W. Blunt White Library, Mystic Seaport Museum, Log 399.

13. Earle, p. 30.

14. "Journal of Sallie G. Smith aboard the Bark *Ohio*," 19 December 1877. G. W. Blunt White Library, Mystic Seaport Museum, Log 399.

15. "Journal of Sallie G. Smith aboard the Bark *Ohio*," 13 September 1877. G. W. Blunt White Library, Mystic Seaport Museum, Log 399.

16. "Journal of Sallie G. Smith aboard the Bark *Ohio*," 14 July 1877. G. W. Blunt White Library, Mystic Seaport Museum, Log 399.

17. Incomplete provenance and an absence of signed pieces complicate the Robinson story.

18. Ashley, p. 115.

19. Wilson, p. 280.

20. Flayderman, p. 164.

21. Flayderman, p. 81.

22. Charles H. Carpenter, "Early Dated Scrimshaw," *Antiques*, 102, no. 3 (September 1972), p. 419.

23. Caron, p. 91.

CHAPTER FIVE

1. Caron, p. 140.

2. For a more complete explanation of current regulations see Gilkerson, pp. 114-117.

3. For a detailed chemical analysis see Janet West, "Scrimshaw: Recent Forgeries in Plastic," *The Mariner's Mirror*, 66 (November 1980), pp. 328-330.

4. Constance P. Ramstedt, "A Method for Differentiating between a Polymer Replica Whale Tooth and a Genuine Whale Tooth," unpublished report, July 1981.

5. Museum correspondence, W. W. Bennett to Carl C. Cutler, 7 February 1947.

6. Author's conversation with William Gilkerson, March 1981.

BIBLIOGRAPHY

Albion, Robert G.; Baker, William A.; and Labaree, Benjamin W. *New England and the Sea*. Middletown, Conn.: Wesleyan University Press, 1972.

American Lloyd's *Registry of American and Foreign Shipping*. New York: 1864-1877.

American Shipmasters' Association. *Record of American and Foreign Shipping*. New York: 1871–.

Ashley, Clifford W. *The Yankee Whaler*. Boston: Houghton Mifflin Co., 1926.

Barbeau, Maurius. "All Hands Aboard Scrimshawing." *American Neptune* 12 (1952): pp. 99-122.

———. "Seafaring Folk Art." *Antiques* 66 (1954): pp. 47-49.

Barnes, Clare. *John F. Kennedy: Scrimshaw Collector*. Boston: Little, Brown & Co., 1969.

Bowen, Abel, comp. *The Naval Monument*. Boston: A. Bowen, 1816.

Caron, Joseph F. "Scrimshaw and Its Importance as an American Folk Art." Ph.D. dissertation, Illinois State University, 1976. Distributed by University Microfilms International, Ann Arbor, Michigan.

Carpenter, Charles H., Jr. "Early Dated Scrimshaw." *Antiques* 102 (1972): pp. 414-419.

Colby, Barnard L. "New London Whaling Captains." The Marine Historical Association, Inc., Publications, 1, no. 1, 1936: pp. 186-225.

Crosby, Everett U. *Susan's Teeth and Much Ado about Scrimshaw*. Nantucket, Mass.: Everett U. Crosby, 1955.

Daland, Edward L. "Engraved Types of Scrimshaw." *Antiques* 28 (1935): pp. 153-155.

Earle, Walter K. *Scrimshaw: Folk Art of the Whalers*. Cold Spring Harbor, New York: Whaling Museum Society, Inc.,1957.

Flayderman, E. Norman. *Scrimshaw and Scrimshanders*. New Milford, Conn.: N. Flayderman & Co., 1972.

Foster, Washington. "Journal of a Voyage Aboard the Schooner *Emeline*, 1843-1844." Old Dartmouth Historical Society Library, New Bedford, Mass.

Gilkerson, William. *The Scrimshander*. Rev. ed. San Francisco: Troubador Press, 1978.

Goode, G. Brown. *The Fisheries and Fishery Industries of the United States*. Washington, D.C.: 1884.

Guldbeck, Per E. *The Care of Historical Collections*. Nashville, Tenn.: American Association for State and Local History, 1972.

Haskins, G. *Narrative of a Global Whaling Voyage 1829-1833*. London: 1839.

Hegarty, Reginald B., comp. *Returns of Whaling Vessels Sailing from American Ports, 1876-1928*. New Bedford, Mass.: Old Dartmouth Historical Society and Whaling Museum, 1959.

Huster, Harrison H. "Scrimshaw: One Part Whalebone, Two Parts Nostalgia." *Antiques* 81 (1961): pp. 122-125.

Isaacson, Philip M. *The American Eagle*. Boston: New York Graphic Society, 1975.

Lloyd's *Register of British and Foreign Shipping*. London: 1834–.

Lord, Priscilla Sawyer, and Foley, Daniel J. *The Folk Arts and Crafts of New England*. Philadelphia: Chilton Books, 1965.

McKenzie, Daniel, Jr. "Journal of a Voyage Aboard the Whaleship *Samuel Robertson*, 1837-1840." Old Dartmouth Historical Society Library, New Bedford, Mass.

Malley, Richard C. "False Teeth: New Problems with Plastic Scrimshaw." *The Log of Mystic Seaport* 32 (1980): pp. 83-89.

Melville, Herman. *Moby-Dick*. New York: Harper & Brothers, 1851.

Merchant Vessels of the U. S. Washington, D. C.: Government Printing Office, 1869–.

Mitchell, Mairin. *The Maritime History of Russia, 1848-1948*. London: Sidgwick and Jackson, Ltd., 1949.

Noyes, Gertrude E. *The Savings Bank of New London*. New London, Conn.: The Savings Bank of New London, 1977.

Olmsted, Francis Allyn. *Incidents of a Whaling Voyage*. New York: D. Appleton and Co., 1841.

"*Orion*, Logbook of the Brig, 1820-1821." G. W. Blunt White Library, Mystic Seaport Museum, Mystic, Conn.

Pentley-Jones, Evan W. "Scrimshaw." *Antiques* 98 (1970): pp. 256-262.

Ramstedt, Constance P. "A Method for Differentiating between a Polymer Replica Whale Tooth and a Genuine Whale Tooth." Unpublished report. Orrington, Maine, 1981.

Ritchie, Carson I. A. *Modern Ivory Carving*. New York: A. S. Barnes and Co., 1972.

Roosevelt, Theodore. *The Naval War of 1812*. New York: G. P. Putnam's Sons, 1910.

Salaman, R. A. *Dictionary of Tools*. New York: Charles Scribner's Sons, 1975.

Scrimshaw, Charles W. Letter in *The Log of Mystic Seaport* 3 (1951): p. 11.

Ship Registers and Enrollments of Bristol-Warren, R. I., 1773-1939. Providence, R. I.: The National Archives Project, 1941.

Ship Registers and Enrollments of New Bedford, Mass., 1796-1939. 3 vols. Boston: The National Archives Project, 1940.

"Ship Registers and Enrollments of New London, Conn." Unpublished report. G. W. Blunt White Library, Mystic Seaport Museum, Mystic, Conn.

Ship Registers and Enrollments of Newport, R. I., 1790-1939. 2 vols. Providence, R. I.: The National Archives Project, 1938-1941.

Smith, Frederick H. "Journal of a Voyage aboard the Bark *Ohio,* 1875-1878." G. W. Blunt White Library, Mystic Seaport Museum, Mystic, Conn.

Smith, Sallie G. "Journal of a Voyage aboard the Bark *John P. West,* 1881-1883." G. W. Blunt White Library, Mystic Seaport Museum, Mystic, Conn.

———. "Journal of a Voyage aboard the Bark *Ohio,* 1875-1878." G. W. Blunt White Library, Mystic Seaport Museum, Mystic, Conn.

Stackpole, Edouard A. *Scrimshaw at Mystic Seaport.* Mystic, Conn.: Marine Historical Association, 1958.

———. *Whales & Destiny.* Amherst: University of Massachusetts Press, 1972.

Starbuck, Alexander. *History of the American Whale Fishery.* 2 vols. 1878. Reprint. New York: Argosy-Antiquarian, Ltd., 1964.

U. S. Navy Department. *Dictionary of American Naval Fighting Ships.* 7 vols. Washington, D. C.: Government Printing Office, 1959-1981.

Watson, Arthur C. *The Long Harpoon.* New Bedford, Mass.: George H. Reynolds, 1929.

West, Janet. "Scrimshaw: Facts and Forgeries." *Antique Collecting* 16 (1982): pp. 17-21.

———. "Scrimshaw: Recent Forgeries in Plastic." *The Mariner's Mirror.* 66 (1980): pp. 328-330.

Whiting, Emma M., and Hough, Henry B. *Whaling Wives.* Boston: Houghton Mifflin Co., 1953.

Wilson, Claggett. "Scrimshaw, the Whaleman's Art." *Antiques* 46 (1946): pp.278-281.

INDEX

Graven by the fishermen themselves

was designed by Klaus Gemming, New Haven, Connecticut.
Finn Typographic Service, Stamford, Connecticut,
set the text in Mergenthaler V-I-P Phototype Galliard,
which was drawn by Matthew Carter, based on typefaces by
the sixteenth-century French type designer Robert Granjon.

The book was printed in fine-screen offset lithography by
The Meriden Gravure Company, Meriden, Connecticut,
on Mohawk Superfine Text paper made by Mohawk Paper Mills,
Cohoes, New York. The color plates were printed on
Lustro Offset Enamel Dull, made by the S. D. Warren
Paper Company, Boston, Massachusetts.

The book was bound by Mueller Trade Bindery,
Middletown, Connecticut.

The objects in the collection were photographed by
Mary Anne Stets and Claire White-Peterson.

Mystic Seaport Museum